S. Hrg. 113–285

THE PARTNERSHIP BETWEEN NIST AND THE PRIVATE SECTOR: IMPROVING CYBERSECURITY

HEARING

BEFORE THE

COMMITTEE ON COMMERCE, SCIENCE, AND TRANSPORTATION UNITED STATES SENATE

ONE HUNDRED THIRTEENTH CONGRESS

FIRST SESSION

JULY 25, 2013

Printed for the use of the Committee on Commerce, Science, and Transportation

U.S. GOVERNMENT PRINTING OFFICE

88–081 PDF   WASHINGTON : 2014

For sale by the Superintendent of Documents, U.S. Government Printing Office
Internet: bookstore.gpo.gov   Phone: toll free (866) 512–1800; DC area (202) 512–1800
Fax: (202) 512–2104   Mail: Stop IDCC, Washington, DC 20402–0001

CONTENTS

THE PARTNERSHIP BETWEEN NIST AND THE PRIVATE SECTOR: IMPROVING CYBERSECURITY

THURSDAY, JULY 25, 2013

U.S. SENATE,
COMMITTEE ON COMMERCE, SCIENCE, AND TRANSPORTATION,
Washington, DC.

The Committee met, pursuant to notice, at 2:37 p.m. in room SR–253, Russell Senate Office Building, Hon. John D. Rockefeller IV, Chairman of the Committee, presiding.

OPENING STATEMENT OF HON. JOHN D. ROCKEFELLER IV, U.S. SENATOR FROM WEST VIRGINIA

The CHAIRMAN. I am going to make a statement, and then Senator Thune is going to make a statement, and then we are going to go right to your testimony because this is a very, very important hearing.

We are going to spend a lot of time today talking about a Federal agency most Americans have never heard up, the National Institute of Standards and Technology, or NIST. I can assure you that in this committee we have heard of NIST. And we understand and appreciate the important role that NIST plays in our country's economic success. You are scientists for one thing. You are engineers. You are technical experts all over the world. The whole technical world and increasingly the public policy world, partly because of cybersecurity but just in general, trusts and knows NIST. You are the worldwide gold standard. That is not me talking. That is other people talking, and you will hear that from the Netherlands in just a second.

So let me give you an example. A couple of weeks ago, this committee was having a hearing on the very important issue of improving forensic science, which is not all that "Law and Order" says that it is. One of our witnesses was the chief of forensic science labs in the Netherlands, which is one of the top forensic science organizations in the world. The Netherlands official proudly announced at the hearing that his agency had just signed a memorandum of agreement with you all at NIST on improving the quality of forensic science standards. When Senator Thune asked him why his agency wanted to partner with NIST, he said it was because when it comes to standards, NIST is, "absolutely the top-notch organization, the state-of-the-art, worldwide."

If you look up NIST's authorizing law, you will read that NIST's core mission is to serve as a laboratory, a science, engineering,

(1)

technology, and measurement laboratory. I really want to stress this point for the members of this committee, those who are here and those who should be, and the business community who may not have worked closely with NIST before, as many of us have. NIST is not a regulatory agency. It is a scientific laboratory to which all sorts and manner of institutions repair to improve themselves.

NIST's mission is to help American businesses solve tough technical problems. Whether it is emerging technologies like the Smart Grid or cloud computing or consumer products like flame-retardant mattresses or television screens, NIST's job is to help American industry help itself. With its unrivaled technical expertise and its well-deserved reputation for objectivity, NIST has been working closely with the private sector for many years to help U.S. companies innovate and to compete with their foreign competitors.

I was very pleased but, frankly, not totally surprised when President Obama issued an executive order earlier this year instructing NIST to begin looking at how we can protect our critical assets from something called "cyber attacks" which, in spite of all we do, Americans seem not to be able to grasp as to their importance and danger. I am looking forward to hearing from Dr. Gallagher and our other witnesses today about how their work on this so-called "Cybersecurity Framework" is progressing.

Getting NIST involved in cybersecurity makes a lot of sense and may save the day for cybersecurity, that is, passing legislation, because NIST already has decades of experience working with the private sector or on computer security issues. NIST's computer security work goes as far back as 1972 when it started working on the Data Encryption Standard.

It also makes sense because we need our country's very best minds in both the public and the private sectors focused on working on this problem. Back in 2009, when Senator Olympia Snowe and I started working on cybersecurity legislation in the Commerce Committee, not everybody appreciated the seriousness of this threat. But today, 4 years later, I believe that we have reached a very broad consensus in this country that cyber attacks present the gravest threats to our national and economic security. The FBI says it. The CIA says it. DOD says it. ODNI says it. Everybody says it. And we just got to drive the point home. And what Senator Thune and I are hoping to do is to do a bill which would actually get this whole process going, the importance of momentum.

But anyway, I think people now do understand cybersecurity represents a huge threat. Every new report about stolen intellectual property or disruption of service attacks against a large U.S. company drives this point home.

Making progress against our cyber adversaries is going to require a sustained, coordinated effort between the public and the private sectors, and it is going to require the combined resources of many different Government agencies, which is part of the problem, and businesses. Acting alone, this committee cannot make all of the changes needed to give our Government and businesses the tools they need to make real progress in cybersecurity because we come from three different jurisdictions, which is not fun. It is OK but it is not the best way to do something.

But there are some important steps that we can and should take such as promoting cybersecurity research and encouraging talented young people to work in cybersecurity, which I think you will agree is a desperate, desperate problem. Probably the most important step we can take as a committee is to make sure that the technical experts at NIST stay engaged and working with the private sector to develop effective cybersecurity standards by which they will stick and do. If this process succeeds, our businesses and the Government agencies will have a powerful new tool to protect ourselves against cybersecurity.

I would like to thank Senator Thune for working with me on this very important issue. Since he became Ranking Member of this committee at the beginning of this year, he has devoted a tremendous amount of time to mastering this whole subject of cybersecurity. Yesterday we introduced legislation that we hope will serve as one of the cornerstones to our country's cybersecurity strategy. I look forward to having a good conversation today about our bill, about other things that we can and should be doing to protect our country from this massive threat.

I thank you.

Senator Thune?

STATEMENT OF HON. JOHN THUNE, U.S. SENATOR FROM SOUTH DAKOTA

Senator THUNE. Thank you, Mr. Chairman, for holding this hearing and for your continued leadership on cybersecurity. You brought this critical issue to the fore, and you have been steadfast in your commitment to addressing the problem.

No one can deny the serious threat that we are confronting in cyberspace. Almost daily we learn of new cyber threats and attacks targeting our Government agencies and the companies that drive our economy. We must find solutions that leverage the innovation and know-how of the private sector, as well as the expertise and information held by the Federal Government. And given the escalating nature of the threat, we should look for solutions that will have both an immediate impact and that will remain flexible and agile into the future.

In keeping with that task, in March this Committee held a joint hearing with the Homeland Security and Governmental Affairs Committee not long after the President issued his cybersecurity Executive Order in February. Today we are here to examine the National Institute of Standards and Technology's implementation of that portion of the Executive Order pertaining to the cybersecurity partnership between the private sector and the Federal Government to improve best practices in cybersecurity. The feedback we have heard from many in the industry regarding NIST's process has been fairly positive so far.

We are also here to examine the legislation that Chairman Rockefeller and I have introduced, after soliciting feedback from industry stakeholders and our colleagues. I think this bill strikes the proper balance to ensure that what develops is industry-led and a true partnership between NIST and the private sector. It also ensures that NIST's involvement and this process are both ongoing in order to maintain the flexibility and continued innovation that is necessary to meet such a dynamic threat.

Our proposed legislation also includes needed titles to improve research and development. We should not underestimate the value of R&D. As I have mentioned previously, I am proud to note that South Dakota's own Dakota State University is one of only four schools in the Nation designated by the National Security Agency as a National Center of Academic Excellence in Cyber Operations. Other titles of our bill improve education and work force development, as well as cybersecurity awareness and preparedness.

I am pleased that our offices worked with industry, fellow Senate colleagues, and other stakeholders to solicit and incorporate their feedback in crafting this legislation and will continue to do so as we move forward. By following regular order in the committees of jurisdiction, we hope to avoid the legislative impasse from the last Congress and ultimately enact legislation that will make real improvements to our nation's cybersecurity.

Our hearing witnesses today include the Director of NIST and representatives from the private sector who can provide this committee with their perspectives on how the current NIST process is developing. I look forward to hearing whether our legislation is a step in the right direction to provide a partnership that is truly voluntary and industry-led.

I am also pleased that the Chairman and I both recognize that an essential component of cybersecurity is strong information sharing regarding threats. Such sharing should occur both between Government and industry and among private sector actors with strong liability protections. It is our hope that our colleagues on the Senate Intelligence Committee will be successful in crafting bipartisan consensus legislation that achieves these goals.

As the Chair of the House Intelligence Committee has said, according to intelligence officials, allowing the Government to share classified information with private companies could stop up to 90 percent of cyber attacks on U.S. networks.

It is also our hope that the Senate Homeland Security Committee can similarly work in a bipartisan fashion to make needed improvements to the Federal Information Security Management Act in order to better secure our Federal networks.

If our Committees can work to produce complementary consensus legislation, that would be a significant step forward in this area.

Again, I thank the Chairman for holding this hearing. I want to thank our witnesses for being here, and we look forward to hearing your testimony. Thank you, Mr. Chairman.

The CHAIRMAN. Thank you, Senator Thune.

I am tempted to ask if any of our other Senators want to say a word, but I just lost that temptation.

[Laughter.]

The CHAIRMAN. So we will start with the Honorable Patrick D. Gallagher, who has been before us recently and frequently. He is Acting Deputy Secretary, Under Secretary of Commerce—I cannot read this stuff—for Standards and Technology, and Director, National Institute of Standards and Technology, U.S. Department of Commerce. I mean, they put the last thing, which is the important thing, last. We did. So I apologize. Anyway, we welcome your statement.

STATEMENT OF DR. PATRICK D. GALLAGHER, UNDER SECRETARY OF COMMERCE FOR STANDARDS AND TECHNOLOGY AND DIRECTOR, NATIONAL INSTITUTE OF STANDARDS AND TECHNOLOGY, UNITED STATES DEPARTMENT OF COMMERCE

Dr. GALLAGHER. Thank you very much. Chairman Rockefeller, Ranking Member Thune, it is a real pleasure to be here and to join you and the rest of this committee to talk about this really important issue. It is great to both be able to talk about NIST, but in particular, I want to talk about this partnership with industry and I want to welcome my colleagues at the table today.

Let me start by mentioning a few words about NIST itself. As you mentioned, since 1901, NIST has played a rather unique and essential role as the Nation's measurement laboratory, as industry's national lab. And in that capacity, it is a nonregulatory agency with the mission to promote U.S. innovation and competitiveness by advancing measurement science, standards, and technology in ways that enhance our economic security and improve our quality of life. And as you will hear more about today, our work in the area of information security, trusted networks, encryption, software quality is applicable to a wide variety of users from small and medium enterprises to large private and public organizations, including agencies of the Federal Government and critical infrastructure companies.

As part of this broader responsibility, on February 13, 2012, the President signed Executive Order 13636 which directed NIST to work with industry to develop a Cybersecurity Framework to improve the cybersecurity of critical infrastructure. We believe that this framework is an important element in addressing the challenges of improving cybersecurity of our critical infrastructure. A NIST-coordinated, but industry-led framework will draw on standards and best practices that industry already develops and uses. NIST will ensure that the process is open and transparent to all stakeholders. We will ensure that there is a robust technical underpinning to the framework, and any effort to better protect critical infrastructure can only work if it is supported and then implemented by the owners and operators of this infrastructure, which are largely in the private sector.

This multi-stakeholder approach leverages the respective strengths of the public and private sectors. It helps develop solutions where both sides will be invested. This approach does not dictate solutions to industry but facilitates industry coming together to develop and offer solutions that the private sector is best positioned to embrace.

Relying on standards which are the result of industry coming together to develop solutions for market needs we believe will give the framework broad acceptance around the world.

Also importantly, the standards have a unique and key attribute of scalability. We can use solutions that are already adopted in industry or if we can readily adopt, then those same solutions, when used by other markets, reduce transactional costs for our businesses. They provide economies of scale which make all of our industries more competitive and make the goal of achieving cybersecurity more doable.

It also reflects the reality that many in the private sector are already doing the right things to protect their systems and should not be diverted from these efforts through new standards.

NIST is engaging with stakeholders through a series of workshops and events to ensure that we can cover the breadth of considerations that will be needed to make this national priority a success. These sessions are designed to identify existing resources, identify gaps, and prioritize the issues that need to be addressed as part of the framework. The workshops also bring together a broad cross section of participants representing critical infrastructure owner/operators, industry associations, standards development organizations, individual companies, government agencies, research labs, and so forth.

Last week, NIST held its third workshop to present initial considerations for the framework. It built a discussion around the draft outline for the preliminary framework that NIST had presented for public review a few weeks prior. This workshop had a particular emphasis on issues that had been identified from the initial work by the public. NIST has gained a consensus on several elements that the framework will include, allowing it to become adaptable, flexibility, and scalable, and to be put into use.

In October, we will have a preliminary framework that builds on these elements.

After the yearlong effort envisioned in the Executive Order, once we have developed this initial framework, the effort will continue. For example, NIST will work with the specific sectors in DHS to build strong, voluntary programs to implement the framework in critical infrastructure areas. That work will then inform the needs of critical infrastructure in the next versions of the framework.

The goal at the end of this process will be for industry to take ownership of the process and update the Cybersecurity Framework themselves, ensuring that the framework will be dynamic and relevant as it continues to evolve.

We have made significant progress. We still have a lot of work to do, and I look forward to working with this committee and with everyone who is participating in the framework process to address the challenges.

And I look forward to the questions and discussion that we will have. Thank you.

[The prepared statement of Dr. Gallagher follows:]

PREPARED STATEMENT OF DR. PATRICK D. GALLAGHER, UNDER SECRETARY OF COMMERCE FOR STANDARDS AND TECHNOLOGY AND DIRECTOR, NATIONAL INSTITUTE OF STANDARDS AND TECHNOLOGY, UNITED STATES DEPARTMENT OF COMMERCE

Introduction

Chairman Rockefeller, Ranking Member Thune, members of the Committee, I am Pat Gallagher, Director of the National Institute of Standards and Technology (NIST), a non-regulatory bureau within the U.S. Department of Commerce. Thank you for this opportunity to testify today on NIST's role under the President's Executive Order 13636, "Improving Critical Infrastructure Cybersecurity" and NIST's responsibility to develop a framework to reduce cyber risks to critical infrastructure.

I want to acknowledge and thank this Committee for its leadership and support on this issue.

The Role of NIST in Cybersecurity

NIST's mission is to promote U.S. innovation and industrial competitiveness by advancing measurement science, standards, and technology in ways that enhance economic security and improve our quality of life. Our work in addressing technical challenges related to national priorities has ranged from projects related to the Smart Grid and electronic health records to atomic clocks, advanced nanomaterials, and computer chips.

In the area of cybersecurity, we have worked with Federal agencies, industry, and academia since 1972 starting with the development of the Data Encryption Standard. Our role to research, develop and deploy information security standards and technology to protect information systems against threats to the confidentiality, integrity and availability of information and services, was strengthened through the Computer Security Act of 1987 and reaffirmed through the Federal Information Security Management Act of 2002.

Consistent with this mission, NIST actively engages with industry, academia, and other parts of the Federal Government including the intelligence community, and elements of the law enforcement and national security communities, coordinating and prioritizing cybersecurity research, standards development, standards conformance demonstration and cybersecurity education and outreach.

Our broader work in the areas of information security, trusted networks, and software quality is applicable to a wide variety of users, from small and medium enterprises to large private and public organizations, including Federal Government agencies and companies involved with critical infrastructure.

Executive Order 13636, "Improving Critical Infrastructure Cybersecurity"

On February 13, 2013, the President signed Executive Order 13636, "Improving Critical Infrastructure Cybersecurity," which gave NIST the responsibility to develop a framework to reduce cyber risks to critical infrastructure (the Cybersecurity Framework). The Executive Order directed NIST to work with industry and develop the Cybersecurity Framework and the Department of Homeland Security (DHS) will establish performance goals. DHS, in collaboration with sector-specific agencies, will support the adoption of the Cybersecurity Framework by owners and operators of critical infrastructure and other interested entities through a voluntary program.

Our partnership with DHS drives much of our effort. Earlier this year, we signed a Memorandum of Agreement with DHS to ensure that our work on the Cybersecurity Framework and the development of cybersecurity standards, best practices, and metrics, is fully integrated with the information sharing, threat analysis, response, and operational work of DHS. We believe this will enable a more holistic approach to address the complex challenges we face.

A Cybersecurity Framework is an important element to address the challenges of improving the cybersecurity of our critical infrastructure. A NIST-coordinated and industry-led Framework will draw on standards and best practices that industry already develops and uses. NIST ensures that the process is open and transparent to all stakeholders including industry, state and local government and academia, and ensures a robust technical underpinning to the Framework. This approach will significantly bolster the Cybersecurity Framework to industry.

This multi-stakeholder approach leverages the respective strengths of the public and private sectors, and helps develop solutions in which both sides will be invested. The approach does not dictate solutions to industry, but rather facilitates industry coming together to offer and develop solutions that the private sector is best positioned to embrace. It also ensures the framework is flexible enough to be applicable to small and mid-sized entities.

I would also like to note that this is not a new or novel approach for NIST. We have utilized similar approaches in the recent past to address other pressing national priorities. For example, NIST's work in the area of Cloud Computing technologies enabled us to develop important definitions and architectures, and is now enabling broad Federal Government deployment of secure Cloud Computing technologies. The lessons learned from this experience and others inform how we plan for and structure our current effort.

Developing the Cybersecurity Framework

The Cybersecurity Framework will consist of standards, methodologies, procedures and processes that align policy, business, and technological approaches to address cyber risks for critical infrastructure. Regulatory agencies will also review the Cybersecurity Framework to determine if current cybersecurity requirements are sufficient, and propose new actions to ensure consistency. Independent regulators are also encouraged to do the same.

This approach reflects both the need for enhancing the security of our critical infrastructure and the reality that the bulk of critical infrastructure is owned and operated by the private sector. Any efforts to better protect critical infrastructure must be supported and implemented by the owners and operators of this infrastructure. It also reflects the reality that many in the private sector are already doing the right things to protect their systems and should not be diverted from those efforts through new requirements.

Current Status of the Cybersecurity Framework and Partnering with Industry

NIST sees its role in developing the Cybersecurity Framework as partnering with industry and other stakeholders to help them develop the Framework. NIST's unique technical expertise in various aspects of cybersecurity related research and technology development, and our established track record of working with a broad cross-section of industry and government agencies in the development of standards and best practices, positions us very well to address this significant national challenge in a timely and effective manner.

NIST's initial steps towards implementing the Executive Order included issuing a Request for Information (RFI) this past February to gather relevant input from industry and other stakeholders, and asking stakeholders to participate in the Cybersecurity Framework process. Given the diversity of sectors in critical infrastructure, the initial efforts are designed to help identify existing cross-sector security standards and guidelines that are applicable to critical infrastructure.

A total of 244 responses were posted on NIST's website. Responses ranged from individuals to large corporations and trade associations and also included comments as brief as a few sentences on specific topics, as well as so comprehensive that they ran over a hundred pages. We published an analysis of these comments in May.

NIST is also engaging with stakeholders through a series of workshops and events to ensure that we can cover the breadth of considerations that will be needed to make this national priority a success. Our first such session—held in April—initiated the process of identifying existing resources and gaps, and prioritized the issues to be addressed as part of the Framework.

At the end of May, a second workshop at Carnegie Mellon University brought together a broad cross-section of participants representing critical infrastructure owners and operators, industry associations, standards developing organizations, individual companies, and government agencies. This three-day working session, using the analysis of the RFI comments as input, was designed to identify and achieve consensus on the standards, guidelines, and practices that will be used in the Framework.

Based on the responses to the RFI, conclusions from the workshops, and NIST analyses, the preliminary Framework is designed and intended:

- To be an adaptable, flexible, and scalable tool for voluntary use;
- To assist in assessing, measuring, evaluating, and improving an organization's readiness to deal with cybersecurity risks;
- To be actionable across an organization;
- To be prioritized, flexible, scalable, performance-based, and cost-effective;
- To rely on standards, guidelines and practices that align with policy, business, and technological approaches to cybersecurity;
- To complement rather than to conflict with current regulatory authorities;
- To promote, rather than to constrain, technological innovation in this dynamic arena;
- To focus on outcomes;
- To raise awareness and appreciation for the challenges of cybersecurity but also the means for understanding and managing the related risks;
- To protect individual privacy and civil liberties; and
- To be built upon national and international standards and other standards, best practices and guidelines that are used globally.

Last week, NIST held its third workshop to present initial considerations for the Framework. This workshop had a particular emphasis on issues that have been identified from the initial work—including the specific needs of different sectors. During the workshop, NIST gained consensus on the elements of the Framework that include:

- A section for senior executives and others on using this Framework to evaluate an organization's preparation for potential cybersecurity-related impacts on their assets and on the organization's ability to deliver products and services. By using this Framework, senior executives can manage cybersecurity risks within their enterprise's business plans and operations.
- A User's Guide to help organizations understand how to apply the Framework.
- Core Sections to address:
  - Five major cybersecurity functions and their categories, subcategories, and informative references;
  - Three Framework Implementation Levels associated with an organization's cybersecurity functions and how well that organization implements the Framework; and
  - A compendium of informative references, existing standards, guidelines, and practices to assist with specific implementation.

At eight months, we will have a preliminary Framework that builds on these elements. In a year's time, once we have developed an initial Framework, there will still be much to do. For example, we will work with specific sectors to build strong voluntary programs for specific critical infrastructure areas. Their work will then inform the needs of critical infrastructure and the next versions of the Framework. The goal at the end of this process will be for industry itself to take "ownership" and update the Cybersecurity Framework.

Conclusion

The cybersecurity challenge facing critical infrastructure is greater than it ever has been. The President's Executive Order reflects this reality, and lays out an ambitious agenda focused on collaboration between the public and private sectors. NIST is mindful of the weighty responsibilities with which we have been charged by President Obama, and we are committed to listening to, and working actively with, critical infrastructure owners and operators to develop a Cybersecurity Framework.

The approach to the Cybersecurity Framework set out in the Executive Order will allow industry to protect our Nation from the growing cybersecurity threat while enhancing America's ability to innovate and compete in a global market. It also helps grow the market for secure, interoperable, innovative products to be used by consumers anywhere.

Thank you for the opportunity to present NIST's views regarding critical infrastructure cybersecurity security challenges. I appreciate the Committee holding this hearing. We have a lot of work ahead of us, and I look forward to working with this Committee and others to help us address these pressing challenges. I will be pleased to answer any questions you may have.

PATRICK D. GALLAGHER

Dr. Patrick Gallagher was confirmed as the 14th Director of the U.S. Department of Commerce's National Institute of Standards and Technology (NIST) on Nov. 5, 2009. He also serves as Under Secretary of Commerce for Standards and Technology, a new position created in the America COMPETES Reauthorization Act of 2010. Prior to his appointment as NIST Director, Gallagher had served as Deputy Director since 2008.

Gallagher provides high-level oversight and direction for NIST. The agency promotes U.S. innovation and industrial competitiveness by advancing measurement science, standards, and technology. NIST's FY 2013 budget includes $778.0 million in direct and transfer appropriations, an estimated $49.7 million in service fees and $120.6 million from other agencies. The agency employs about 3,000 scientists, engineers, technicians, support staff, and administrative personnel at two main locations in Gaithersburg, Md., and Boulder, Colo. NIST also hosts about 2,700 associates from academia, industry, and other government agencies, who collaborate with NIST staff and access user facilities. In addition, NIST partners with more than 1,300 manufacturing specialists and staff at more than 400 MEP service locations around the country.

Under Gallagher, NIST has greatly expanded its participation, often in a leadership role, in collaborative efforts between government and the private sector to address major technical challenges facing the Nation. NIST's participation in these efforts stems from the agency's long history of technical accomplishments and leadership in private-sector led standards-development organizations and in research fields such as manufacturing engineering, cybersecurity and computer science, forensic science, and building and fire science. Currently, he co-chairs the Standards Subcommittee under the White House National Science and Technology Council.

Gallagher joined NIST in 1993 as a research physicist and instrument scientist at the NIST Center for Neutron Research (NCNR), a national user facility for neutron scattering on the NIST Gaithersburg campus. In 2000, he became group leader for facility operations, and in 2004 he was appointed NCNR Director. In 2006, the U.S. Department of Commerce awarded Gallagher a Gold Medal, its highest honor, for his leadership in interagency coordination efforts.

Gallagher received his Ph.D. in physics at the University of Pittsburgh and a bachelor's degree in physics and philosophy from Benedictine College.

The CHAIRMAN. Thank you, sir. Thank you very much.
Now Mr. Arthur W. Coviello, Jr. Did I get that right?
Mr. COVIELLO. You did.
The CHAIRMAN. Thank you. Who is Executive Chairman, RSA, The Security Division of EMC. That is a form of encryption.

STATEMENT OF ARTHUR W. COVIELLO, JR., EXECUTIVE CHAIRMAN, RSA, THE SECURITY DIVISION OF EMC

Mr. COVIELLO. Yes. We are the gold standard of encryption actually.
The CHAIRMAN. OK.
Mr. COVIELLO. So thank you, Chairman Rockefeller and Ranking Member Thune and members of the Committee. I am pleased to have the opportunity to address you today regarding NIST's partnership with industry in the area of cybersecurity.

RSA is a leading provider of not just encryption technology, but other security compliance and risk management solutions for organizations worldwide. We do help the world's leading organizations succeed in their efforts in IT infrastructure by solving their most complex and sensitive security challenges.

Today's hearing topic is one that is close to home for our company. EMC and RSA have already enjoyed a close partnership with NIST. We work closely with Dr. Gallagher and his team on a number of issues that are tightly linked to information security. From our vantage point as a provider of security solutions, RSA's collaboration with NIST is at the heart of our collective goal of safeguarding the world from an advanced and evolving cyber threat.

NIST's National Cybersecurity Center of Excellence Lab initiative offers U.S. companies a valuable opportunity to collaborate with NIST to address a range of security risks and privacy protection imperatives. I repeat also "privacy protection imperatives." With the goal of securing critical infrastructure, the center inspires technological innovation to find creative solutions to intractable and growing cybersecurity challenges.

Of late, EMC and RSA, along with other private sector companies, have appreciated the opportunity to work closely with NIST on implementing the President's Executive Order. Through a collaborative effort to develop a Cybersecurity Framework for critical infrastructure, we have worked with stakeholders to explore the art of the possible to bring our nation to the cutting edge of cybersecurity. This collaboration between industry and NIST is a great example of what the public and private sectors can do together and represents an important step in the right direction.

However, your legislation is still needed to create a more effective, long-term partnership between the public and private sectors. So we applaud the Committee for its work to develop bipartisan legislation based on an industry-driven, voluntary approach. The Cybersecurity Act of 2013 complements the President's executive order by codifying the important steps the administration has already taken to protect critical infrastructure and gives Government and industry additional tools to bolster our cyber defenses.

As efforts progress, we urge you to consider three key points.

First, any successful cybersecurity effort should be industry-driven, as you have done. With the rapid pace of innovation, owners and operators of critical infrastructure are the ones best positioned to keep pace with the rapidly evolving, and sometimes equally innovative, threat landscape. For this reason, standards and best practices should be nonprescriptive, nonregulatory, and technology neutral. Things move too fast. This legislation achieves those objectives by initiating a voluntary, industry-led standards development process that will build on the great work that is already being done in the private sector. This close and continuous coordination between Government and industry is vital to the ongoing development of best practices to combat these ever-changing threats. A common understanding supported by NIST can enable us collectively to move farther and faster in our race against the threat actors.

Second, as we move forward, we must think not only of today's threats but also of the cybersecurity challenges of the future. That is why we are pleased to see that the legislation includes provisions to increase cybersecurity research and to support the development of the cybersecurity workforce. Investments in cybersecurity education and workforce training today will develop the talent we need to strengthen our defenses for years to come. And I can tell you the shortage of skilled people in the industry is one of our most critical problems.

I can also tell you with the rapidly evolving pace of technology adoption and all the great productivity that can be derived from implementing information technology, the attack surface is only going to expand dramatically. We will only be able to take advantage of these great technology innovations if people have confidence. That is why the framework that is being developed in cooperation with the private sector and NIST is so important to our future; this will be an ongoing problem.

And third, as both Chairman Rockefeller and Ranking Member Thune have pointed out, it is imperative that Congress address other key cybersecurity issues not under this committee's jurisdiction. Removing barriers and promoting the safe and secure sharing of actionable threat intelligence between the public and private sectors will enhance our collective ability to mitigate future threats.

Additionally, we must modernize Federal information security management, standardize breach notification, and streamline the acquisition of technology in order to create a positive business climate, while improving our nation's cybersecurity posture.

So, once again, we thank Chairman Rockefeller and Ranking Member Thune for their dedication to advancing this important legislation. I strongly believe the actions undertaken by this committee and the bipartisan leadership of its members will set a positive course for others in Congress to realize the urgency in addressing this growing threat. As the Senate confronts the policy challenges of cybersecurity, I have every confidence in industry's ability to leverage its existing relationship with NIST to enhance the cybersecurity of our critical infrastructure. Under this committee's leadership, we sincerely hope that Congress will act quickly to address this urgent threat to our national security.

I look forward to working with you and your colleagues in Congress as this proposal advances. And again, I thank you for the opportunity to be here today, and I look forward to your questions. Thank you.

[The prepared statement of Mr. Coviello follows:]

PREPARED STATEMENT OF ARTHUR W. COVIELLO, JR., EXECUTIVE CHAIRMAN, RSA, THE SECURITY DIVISION OF EMC

Introduction

Chairman Rockefeller, Ranking Member Thune, and Members of the Committee, my name is Art Coviello and I am an Executive Vice President of EMC Corporation and Executive Chairman of RSA, The Security Division of EMC. Thank you for the opportunity to testify today regarding the National Institute of Standards and Technology (NIST)'s work with industry in the area of cybersecurity. Today's hearing topic is one that is close to home for our company. EMC and RSA have enjoyed a partnership with NIST that has spanned decades, and we are pleased to be working with them today to enhance our nation's cybersecurity.

RSA provides security, compliance, and risk management solutions for organizations worldwide. We help the world's leading organizations succeed by solving their most complex and sensitive security challenges, making it possible for them to safely benefit from the tremendous opportunities of digital technology and the Internet. EMC Corporation is a global leader in enabling businesses and third-party providers to transform their operations and deliver Information Technology (IT) as a service through innovations in big data, cloud computing and data storage.

The United States, like many other nations, is highly dependent upon IT. Everything from national security and intelligence, to commerce and business, to personal communications and social networking depends on networked systems. The dynamic nature of this sector has created millions of jobs and generated significant economic growth. Every day, the Internet is increasing productivity; driving globalization and political change; and fueling every major industry and economy in the world.

Unfortunately, that same dynamism has given rise to an ever-evolving cyber threat that threatens every individual, every company, every industry, and every country in the networked world.

The recent rise in cyber attacks is nothing short of astounding. According to the Government Accountability Office (GAO), the number of cyber attacks reported by Federal agencies increased by 782 percent from Fiscal Year 2006 to Fiscal Year 2012, from 5,503 to 48,562.[1] Clearly, our government is under attack, and those statistics do not account for the daily intrusions private sector entities and private citizens are facing from a wide range of threat actors.

As a provider of security solutions, we are seeing first-hand the rapid evolution of the threat landscape, with more varied targets, and in many cases, more advanced technologies and tactics than ever before. This ever-increasing risk is threatening to erode trust in digital commerce, communication and collaboration on which we have all come to depend.

I have been involved in the policy debates regarding information security and privacy for a number of years, and I appreciate this Committee's sustained leadership on these issues. Given its potential for loss and disruption, cybersecurity has become a vital economic and national security issue, and we applaud the Committee for its work to reach a bipartisan solution.

---

[1] GAO, *Cybersecurity: A Better Defined and Implemented Strategy is Needed to Address Persistent Challenges*, GAO 13 462T (Washington, D.C.: March 7, 2013).

Partnership with NIST

EMC and RSA have long enjoyed a close partnership with NIST on a number of issues that are closely linked to information security. As a provider of security solutions, RSA's collaboration with NIST is at the heart of our collective goal of safeguarding the networked world from an advanced and evolving cyber threat. NIST's National Cybersecurity Center of Excellence (NCCoE) lab initiative offers U.S. companies a valuable opportunity to collaborate with NIST and the public sector to address a range of security risks and privacy protection imperatives. With a goal of securing critical infrastructure, the Center inspires technological innovation to find creative solutions to intractable cybersecurity challenges.

Director Gallagher and the NIST team have been exceptional partners with industry. Since the President announced in February his Executive Order "Improving Critical Infrastructure Cybersecurity," we have been working with other stakeholders and NIST to develop a voluntary framework for reducing cyber risks to critical infrastructure that references standards, guidelines, and best practices to promote the protection of critical infrastructure. We have also partnered with NIST in its NCCoE lab initiative to address a range of security risks in support of the National Cybersecurity Excellence Partnership (NCEP). As a public-private partnership, the NCEP offers U.S. companies the opportunity to form a long-term relationship with the NCCoE. Through a collaborative effort, participating companies work together to explore the "art of the possible" and bring our nNation to the cutting edge of cybersecurity. The NCCoE's strategy is focused on and driven by the practical cybersecurity needs of American businesses, which is a secure cyber infrastructure that inspires technological innovation and fosters economic growth.

Collaboration among innovators provides real-world cybersecurity capabilities that address business needs and help people secure their data and digital infrastructure by equipping them with practical ways to implement cost-effective, repeatable and scalable cybersecurity solutions. It also enables companies to rapidly adopt commercially-available cybersecurity technologies by reducing their total cost of ownership. Most importantly, it empowers innovators to creatively address businesses' most pressing cybersecurity challenges in a state-of-the-art, collaborative environment.[2]

RSA's "Archer" solution is one example this collaborative effort. Incorporated into the NCCoE's geo-location and security profiling environments, Archer allows adaptation to compliance requirements involving privacy, international safe harbor restrictions and applications in the cloud.

As a multinational corporation that operates in over 80 countries around the world, we favor global standards whenever possible. The use of international standards is critical as we seek to meet the broad needs of our user base, but these standards must again be industry-led, voluntary and non-prescriptive. If developed in a transparent, flexible manner, international standards make it possible for global organizations and their customers to continue to make improvements as needs change.

Even so, we recognize that in some cases NIST must develop new standards for Federal Government nonclassified information systems. In these cases, we urge NIST to continue to work in an open, transparent process with stakeholder input. Here are a few examples of our ongoing engagement with NIST around standards development and use:

- RSA's BSAFE product is validated against FIPS 140–2 on a regular basis to ensure our cryptographic implementations. It is our understanding that NIST made a significant contribution from their FIPS 140–2 work to the development of the complementary international standard for cryptographic modules.[3]

- NIST cited EMC's contributions to a NIST Interagency Report on supply chain (NIST IR 7622) as we offered detailed, constructive suggestions over several years to improve the document.[4]

- An RSA employee coauthored a (Draft) NIST Interagency Report: *Trusted Geolocation in the Cloud: Proof of Concept Implementation* (NIST IR 7904 Draft).[5]

- EMC works closely with our Federal customers to help them assess the risks of their new proposed information systems following the Federal Information Security Management Act (FISMA) process. The risk-based FISMA process,

---

[2] *http://csrc.nist.gov/nccoe/The-Center/Mission/Strategy.html*
[3] ISO/IEC 19790: Information technology—Security techniques—Security requirements for cryptographic modules
[4] *http://nvlpubs.nist.gov/nistpubs/ir/2012/NIST.IR.7622.pdf*
[5] *http://csrc.nist.gov/publications/drafts/ir7904/draft_nistir_7904.pdf*

which itself deserves further updating, is in turn anchored in NIST standards such as the recently updated NIST 800–53 Rev 4 security control catalog.[6] We appreciate that this new security catalog has a detailed mapping to two key international standards in wide industry use: ISO 27001[7] and The Common Criteria.[8] For the first time, this prominent U.S. Federal standard outlines controls for privacy along with security, a key linkage that we were pleased to see acknowledged in your draft legislation.

EMC/RSA as an Industry Leader

In addition to our longstanding history working with NIST, EMC, and RSA have a proven track record as an industry leader in security. RSA has long recognized that cybersecurity is dynamic, and all stakeholders must continue to evolve our collective ability to counter cyber threats. In 1991, we responded to this new challenge by creating one of the largest security thought-leadership conferences in the world, RSA Conference. It is an annual industry event, which seeks to help drive the global information security agenda. Throughout its history, RSA Conference has consistently attracted the best and brightest in the field, creating opportunities for conference attendees to learn about IT security's most important issues through firsthand interactions with peers, luminaries and both established and emerging companies. As the IT security field continues to grow in importance and influence, RSA Conference, in conjunction with our many industry partners, plays an integral role in keeping security professionals across the globe connected and educated.

EMC/RSA has demonstrated a longstanding commitment to improving our industry's best practices, particularly in the secure development field. In 2007, EMC, along with other industry leaders, created the Software Assurance Forum for Excellence in Code (SAFECode) to define, promote and share best practices and guidance outlining how to build secure software. SAFECode represents the first coherent, user-friendly collection of industry best practices in the development space. Available to the public free of charge, SAFECode's best practice guidance documents outline realistic approaches to secure development.[9] The SAFECode initiative has produced a wealth of accumulated knowledge and shareable training materials that are being leveraged every day by developers to create software that is more secure than anything we have seen before.

RSA knows first hand that no one is immune to the cyber threat. In 2011, RSA detected a targeted cyber attack on our systems. Certain information related to an RSA product had been extracted. We publicly disclosed the breach and immediately began working to develop and publish best practices and remediation steps, so that others could learn from our experience. We proactively reached out to thousands of customers across the public and private sectors to help them mitigate the effects of the breach. Further, we worked with the appropriate U.S. Federal government agencies, including NIST, and several information sharing and analysis centers (ISACs) to ensure broad communication of these best practices and remediation steps, as well as information about the attack.

Our experience was not unique. Individuals, governments, and companies deal with threats every day from nation states, criminals, hacktivists, and rogue actors. We have made great strides in the security space, but there is much work left to be done. As Robert Bigman, former CISO of the Central Intelligence Agency (CIA), has stated, the United States is "exactly where the cyber criminals want us to be. They're very happy with our current situation."[10]

The cyber threats we collectively face are real and immediate, and there are a number of steps that must be taken to enhance our economic and national security.

Implementing the President's Executive Order

Recently, EMC and RSA, along with other private sector companies, have appreciated the opportunity to work closely with NIST on the implementation of the President's Executive Order to Improve Critical Infrastructure Cybersecurity.

This collaboration between industry and NIST is a great example of what the public and private sectors can do together and represents an important step in the right direction. However, legislation is still needed to create a more effective partnership between the public and private sectors.

---

[6] *http://nvlpubs.nist.gov/nistpubs/SpecialPublications/NIST.SP.800-53r4.pdf*
[7] ISO/IEC 27001: Information technology–Security techniques–Information security management systems–Requirements
[8] ISO/IEC 15408: Information technology—Security techniques—Evaluation criteria for IT security
[9] SAFECode.org/publications
[10] *http://www.usnews.com/news/articles/2012/12/04/former-cia-officer-united-states-lags-far-behind-in-cyber-security*

Key Elements of the Draft Legislation

We applaud the Committee for its work to develop bi-partisan legislation based on an industry-driven, voluntary approach. This legislation complements the President's Executive Order by codifying the important steps the Administration has already taken to protect critical infrastructure and gives government and industry additional tools to bolster our cyber defenses. We are pleased to see that the draft bill requires a voluntary, non-regulatory process, enabling further collaboration between the public and private sectors to leverage non-prescriptive and technology-neutral, global cybersecurity standards for critical infrastructure. We also commend the Committee for including crucial provisions to support cyber research and development; increase awareness of cyber risks; and improve cybersecurity education and workforce training.

As efforts progress, we urge you to consider a few key points:

(1) Any successful cybersecurity effort must be industry-driven.

With the rapid pace of innovation, owners and operators of critical infrastructure need the flexibility to keep pace with the rapidly-evolving and sometimes equally innovative threat landscape. For this reason, standards and best practices should be non-prescriptive, non-regulatory, and technology-neutral. This draft legislation achieves those objectives by initiating a voluntary, industry-led standards development process that will build on the great work that is already being done in the private sector. This close and continuous coordination between government and industry is vital to the ongoing development of best practices to combat the ever-changing threats we all face.

Collaborative efforts between government and industry have been similarly successful in addressing supply chain security issues. EMC has been an early adopter of industry best practices to strengthen the security of our supply chain and ensure the global integrity of our software and hardware development processes. EMC shared its experience in two SAFECode whitepapers on software integrity.[11] As a leader in the security field, RSA has actively engaged with government and industry partners to develop global supply chain security standards.

The following are a few examples of industry-led efforts to develop and implement security standards:

The Common Criteria: The Common Criteria [12] are a set of international computer security standards developed by governments that include Canada, France, Germany, the Netherlands, the United Kingdom and the United States through active engagement with industry. EMC/RSA has made substantial investments over many years to certify many of our products against the Common Criteria, which are now recognized by 26 countries. U.S. policy should encourage those countries that do not yet recognize The Common Criteria to follow suit as a baseline assessment and avoid separate, custom national evaluations in order to access their markets.

Protection Profiles: Industry has taken the lead to contribute technical content related to supply chain evaluations against standard "Protection Profiles" for different classes of technology. This directly supports a strategy by The Common Criteria Development Board and the National Security Agency (NSA)'s National Information Assurance Partnership (NIAP) unit to reorient product evaluations towards protection profiles, many of which are also developed by industry.

Open Trusted Technology Provider Standard (O–TTPS): In 2009, RSA's Chief Technology Officer worked with the U.S. Department of Defense to launch a joint public-private initiative that led to a published global supply chain standard in April 2013. The resulting standard, The Open Group's O–TTPS Standard for *Mitigating Maliciously Tainted and Counterfeit Products* [13] addresses two of our most important threats. Earlier this month at their international conference, The Open Group's Trusted Technology Forum awarded EMC for its "outstanding contribution" to this multi-year standard development process. The new, global O–TTPS standard will have a measurable accreditation program by year's end, enabling compliance down into the technology supply chain. This non-prescriptive pilot program focuses on measuring the outcomes of practices, while giving each organization the latitude to determine how best to reach the

---

[11] SAFECode.org/publications
[12] ISO/IEC 15408: Information technology—Security techniques—Evaluation criteria for IT security—Part 1: Introduction and general model
[13] *http://www.opengroup.org/news/press/open-group-releases-global-technology-supply-chain-security-standard*

performance goals. This Open Group industry standards effort also has a formal liaison with ISO/IEC's emerging standard on supplier relationships that has itself been developed with significant industry review and comments.[14]

(2) Public and private sector collaboration is essential to bolstering cybersecurity.

EMC and RSA strongly support the bill's aim of establishing more effective collaboration between industry and government to address cybersecurity issues. We already participate in two successful initiatives that we believe can serve as a model for future public-private partnerships in the cybersecurity field.

At the national level, the Enduring Security Framework (ESF) is a partnership of senior industry and government executives to identify critical cyber vulnerabilities and mobilize experts to address the risks. At the regional level, the New England Advanced Cyber Security Center is a consortium of industry, government, and universities working together to share cyber threats and explore new areas of research required to improve our defenses.

(3) Cybersecurity standards should be voluntary, non-prescriptive, and technology-neutral.

The voluntary nature of the legislation is of paramount importance. While we support the development of standards and best practices, we firmly believe that companies should have the flexibility to determine for themselves how best to secure their networks. In this highly-innovative sector, companies need the flexibility to explore creative approaches and technologies. Government regulations cannot reasonably keep pace with innovation, and companies must be free to design and build secure products in a global environment as they see fit without government intrusion. This ensures ongoing technology innovation in a global marketplace, resulting in increased productivity, job creation, and economic growth.

(4) Both government and the private sector must invest in increasing public awareness of the cyber threat.

In today's increasingly interconnected world, every individual has a role to play in enhancing cybersecurity. As we have seen, simple errors such as the use of weak passwords and poor cyber hygiene can have serious consequences. For this reason, we strongly support the legislation's call for NIST to launch a cybersecurity awareness campaign. Increased awareness is our first line of defense against cyber attacks, and we applaud the Committee for recognizing this. As NIST undertakes this effort, there are a number of existing public-private partnerships upon which we can build.

The National Cyber Security Alliance (NCSA) is a non-profit organization comprised of captains of industry ranging from defense and IT companies to financial institutions and e-commerce providers to telecommunications companies and ISPs. Founded in 2001, the Alliance works with all levels of government to promote cybersecurity awareness. As one its founding members, EMC/RSA has been involved in this partnership since its inception and as the cybersecurity challenge has grown, so has the Alliance.[15]

In collaboration with its public sector partners, NCSA established National Cyber Security Month in October, which is designed to elevate and expand cybersecurity awareness programs. We appreciate the support of the President of the United States and the U.S. Congress in this effort, and we are pleased to see that the initiative has grown year after year. The U.S. Department of Homeland Security (DHS) is a long-time participant and supporter of this public-private partnership as are multiple other Federal government agencies and many state and local governments.

NCSA has also partnered with the Anti-Phishing Working Group (APWG) and DHS to launch the Stop-Think-Connect awareness campaign; an effort we will continue supporting actively to help grow its influence as a nationwide and multi-national public awareness initiative.[16]

(5) As we move forward, we must think not only of today's threats, but also of the cybersecurity challenges of the future.

Today, thousands of cybersecurity positions remain unfilled in both the public and private sectors, simply because of a lack of qualified candidates. We are pleased to

---

[14] ISO/IEC 27036: Information technology—Security techniques—Information security for supplier relationships—Part 1: Overview and concepts
[15] *www.staysafeonline.org*
[16] *http://stopthinkconnect.org/*

see that the draft legislation includes provisions to increase cybersecurity research and to support the development of the cybersecurity workforce.

Title II of the draft legislation calls for a national cybersecurity research and development plan to be developed by the Office of Science and Technology Policy (OSTP) and the coordination of research and development activities at the National Science Foundation (NSF), NIST, other Federal agencies, academia, and the private sector. We believe the authorization of coordinated research will address gaps in knowledge that prevent the development of secure technologies. In addition, the Networking and Information Technology Research and Development (NITRD) program has been successful in supporting research on the science of cybersecurity and will enhance the continuation of innovative approaches to new technology.

Title III of the draft bill supports efforts to prepare the cybersecurity workforce of tomorrow. Our young people are our greatest asset, but our students are falling behind in the crucial fields of science, technology, engineering and math. Investments in cybersecurity education and workforce training today will develop the talent we need to strengthen our defenses for years to come.

As cyber threats continue to escalate at an alarming rate, we need to invest in building the cybersecurity workforce with the requisite skills to defend our systems and drive continued innovation. Two areas of investment are particularly important:

Cyber security programs in post-secondary schools: To defend our networks, we will need to graduate more individuals with expertise in computer sciences, risk assessment, data mining, data visualization and analytics, digital forensics, and human behavior. Our colleges and universities must place an emphasis on producing graduates with the technical and cross-functional skills needed to defend against our cyber adversaries. The Federal government should support programs at the college and university levels that graduate qualified cybersecurity professionals. One such example is the Scholarship for Service program, funded by NSF, NSA and DHS, which has produced cybersecurity professionals now working in both the public and private sectors.[17] This and other successful government-funded scholarship programs should be expanded to continue to grow the cyber workforce.

Training, certification and accreditation programs to increase and maintain cybersecurity proficiency: In 2009, SAFECode members outlined a framework around secure engineering training that concluded that they could not sufficiently rely on colleges and universities to deliver graduates that could join the workforce without substantial, advanced company-led training.[18] Consequently, government and private enterprises should provide increased cybersecurity training opportunities for their IT staff. The SANS Institute and the International Information System Security Certification Consortium (ISC2) and Information Systems Audit and Control Association (ISACA) provide education and certification programs that can be replicated and expanded to further develop the cyber workforce.

In addition, new programs such as the U.S. Cyber Challenge[19] and the National Initiative for Cybersecurity Education (NICE) should serve as models for future education programs. NICE has evolved from the Comprehensive National Cybersecurity Initiative, and extends its scope beyond the Federal workplace to include civilians and students in kindergarten through post-graduate school.[20] The goal of NICE is to establish an operational, sustainable and continually improving cybersecurity education program to enhance the Nation's security. These vitally important initiatives are being put into place to identify, recruit and place the next generation of cybersecurity professionals.

This effort will require significant investments today, but if these initiatives are implemented properly, our technological future is bright. We look forward to a time when government and industry work as true partners to combat cyber threats. We also look forward to having a skilled and savvy workforce that comes to the table understanding the threat landscape and best practices ready to apply their expertise in a rich economic environment. These cyber professionals will be the brightest and best-trained that we have ever seen, and they will develop innovative ways to combat the cyber threats more quickly and more creatively than we could ever dream of today.

[17] *https://www.sfs.opm.gov/*
[18] SAFECode.org/publications
[19] For more information, go to the U.S. Cyber Challenge Website at: *http://workforce.cisecurity.org/.*
[20] *http://csrc.nist.gov/nice/aboutUs.html*

For all of the reasons noted above, this draft legislation represents an important step in the right direction, but there is more work yet to be done.

Next Steps

In order to effectively address cyber threats there must be an "innovative and cooperative approach between the private sector and the Federal government" and we need to collectively utilize expertise within both government and industry. As Commander of U.S. Cyber Command General Keith Alexander has said many times, "securing our nation's network is a team sport." [21] Without strong public-private partnerships and actionable cyber intelligence information sharing between government and industry, we will not be able to make the progress that is so desperately needed. Moving forward, we recommend two key next steps:

(1) Government should explore additional opportunities to leverage public-private partnerships.

We greatly appreciate NIST's commitment to working with industry, and we believe similar public-private partnerships should be explored. The public sector should further leverage information available from commercial services to paint a fuller picture of the threat landscape.

For example, the RSA Anti-Fraud Command Center (AFCC) has worked globally with financial institutions, ISPs, law enforcement and other organizations to detect and shut down hundreds of thousands of phishing attacks since 2007.[22]

Similarly, we have worked with industry-led Information Sharing Analysis Centers (ISACs) that are partnering with government entities and law enforcement—such as the Financial Services ISAC—to provide timely and actionable information on cyber threats and attacks.[23] Actionable information gained from these mechanisms and in other processes with industry is often as valuable as information from government sources.

(2) It is imperative that Congress addresses other key cybersecurity issues not under this Committee's jurisdiction.

These include advancing the sharing of cyber threat intelligence between government and industry; establishing liability protections for entities that share threat information; and streamlining acquisition of technology. We urge the Congress to examine ways to break down barriers to information sharing and create incentives for the public and private sectors to work together to safely and securely share real-time, actionable information about cyber threats. Linking the adoption of cybersecurity standards to incentives such as liability protection and streamlined acquisition of technology will create a positive business climate while improving our nation's cybersecurity posture.

We also support additional legislative initiatives to update criminal laws and penalties; enact Federal data breach law; modernize FISMA; and develop reasonable and effective policy approaches to supply chain protection that will not stifle innovation and competition.

Conclusion

We thank Chairman Rockefeller and Ranking Member Thune for their dedication to advancing this important legislation. I strongly believe the action undertaken by this Committee and the bipartisan leadership of its Members will set a positive course for others in Congress to realize the urgency in addressing this growing threat. As the Senate confronts the policy challenges of cybersecurity, I have every confidence in industry's ability to leverage its existing relationship with NIST to enhance the cybersecurity of our critical infrastructure. Under this Committee's leadership, we sincerely hope that Congress will act quickly to address this urgent threat to our national security.

Again, I thank you for the opportunity to be here today, and EMC and RSA look forward to working with you and your colleagues in Congress as this proposal advances.

---

[21] http://365.rsaconference.com/community/archive/usa/blog/2011/02/17/video-rsac-us-2011-keynote-the-department-of-defense-active-cyber-defense-and-the-secure-zone__general-keith-b-alexander

[22] For more information on the AFCC, see http://www.emc.com/collateral/solution-overview/10580-afcc-sb.pdf

[23] For more information on the FS–ISAC's information sharing practices and programs, see "Testimony of William B. Nelson, The Financial Services Information Sharing & Analysis Center" before the U.S. House of Representatives Financial Institutions and Consumer Credit Subcommittee, September 14, 2011.

19

The CHAIRMAN. Thank you, sir, very much.

At 3:15, there will likely be a vote, and I just need to inform members of that because I just found out. That is what happens in the Senate. So we will just disappear. If we can stage it, we will do that so we keep the hearing going.

All right. Mark Clancy, Managing Director, Technology Risk Management and Corporate Information Security Officer, The Depository Trust & Clearing Corporation. Please, sir.

STATEMENT OF MARK G. CLANCY, MANAGING DIRECTOR, THE DEPOSITORY TRUST & CLEARING CORPORATION ON BEHALF OF THE AMERICAN BANKERS ASSOCIATION, FINANCIAL SERVICES ROUNDTABLE, AND SECURITIES INDUSTRY AND FINANCIAL MARKETS ASSOCIATION

Mr. CLANCY. Thank you. Chairman Rockefeller, Ranking Member Thune, and members of the Committee, thank you for scheduling today's hearing on improving cybersecurity through the NIST and private sector partnership.

My name is Mark Clancy and I am the Corporate Information Security Officer of the Depository Trust & Clearing Corporation, or DTCC. I also have leadership roles in the Financial Services Sector Coordinating Council and the Financial Services Information Sharing Analysis Center, which is the operational hub for information sharing in the financial sector.

DTCC is participant-owned, governed, and serves the critical infrastructure for the U.S. and global capital markets. DTCC provides many services to the financial industry, but the easiest way to think about us is with one example. After a trade is executed on a stock exchange, we ensure that the shares move to the people who bought them and the money moves to the people who sold them. We do this across all the major exchanges in the United States, and in the aggregate, DTCC processed last year $1.6 quadrillion in transactions and all of that occurred in cyberspace.

Today I am testifying on behalf of the American Bankers Association, the Financial Services Roundtable, the Securities Industry and Financial Markets Association who collectively represent a large segment of the financial services sector. We applaud and support the goals of the bill crafted by the leadership of the Committee.

Researchers estimate there is $100 billion in annual loss to the U.S. economy and half a million jobs lost as a result of cyber crime and cyber espionage.

The financial sector institutions perform risk assessments based on the types of attacks and threat actors that we are subjected to. We group threat actors into four categories: crime, hacktivism, espionage, and war. The threats from these groups range from theft of customer information or intellectual property through disruptions such as denial of service attacks to the destruction of systems and data.

The financial services sector recognizes cybersecurity is a noncompetitive area and is committed to working together to address this issue. A key organization in this partnership is the Financial Services Coordinating Council whose mission is to strengthen the resiliency of the financial services sector against attacks and other threats of the Nation's critical infrastructure.

We appreciate and support the goals of S. 1353 for NIST to facilitate the necessary private and public sector collaboration to establish voluntary standards and best practices to better secure our nation from cyber attack. The sector believes strongly that to be successful, the collaboration must include the leadership in the private and public sector, as well as industry practitioners who address cybersecurity-related risks every day. The frameworks and standards that are rooted in the global, real-world, real-time nature of the threat are those that will achieve the objectives of the Nation to reduce risk from cyber threats to critical infrastructure.

The sector has participated in a number of NIST initiatives over the years and has found the organization to be ideal for the development of standards and collaboration. Supporting the development of the NIST Cybersecurity Framework has been a major initiative of the sector. We provided comments to NIST with an emphasis on the existing national and international regulatory frameworks that the sector currently complies with. We have actively participated in the workshops and are appreciative of the efforts by NIST to seek the sector's input on specific topics and to understand how the Cybersecurity Framework will be used by our sector.

The Committee bill incorporates this collaborative effort, and we hope to see swift passage of the bill. I wanted to highlight four major issues of interest in the bill to the financial services sector.

One, NIST as the Government organization with the responsibility to develop standards.

Two, increasing research and development for the design and testing of software.

Three, educating the workforce and preparing students for future technical roles.

And four, promoting a national cybersecurity awareness campaign.

There are two additional points Congress should consider as this bill is finalized.

First, we strongly encourage the research agenda to include the evaluation of risk management through the supply chain. This will improve the resilience of all sectors by detecting and defending against software and hardware components that have been tampered with during the production, shipment, and through the international supply chain process.

Second, in addition to this bill, we encourage the Senate to introduce and pass legislation that would enhance the ability of the private sector and Government to share cyber threat information while providing the necessary privacy protections for individuals.

On behalf of the American Bankers Association, the Financial Services Roundtable, the Securities Industry and Financial Markets Association, along with DTCC, I would like to thank you for holding today's hearing to continue to raise awareness on this critical issue and for inviting us to testify. I would be happy to address any questions that you may have.

[The prepared statement of Mr. Clancy follows:]

PREPARED STATEMENT OF MARK G. CLANCY, MANAGING DIRECTOR, THE DEPOSITORY TRUST & CLEARING CORPORATION ON BEHALF OF THE AMERICAN BANKERS ASSOCIATION, FINANCIAL SERVICES ROUNDTABLE, AND SECURITIES INDUSTRY AND FINANCIAL MARKETS ASSOCIATION

Chairman Rockefeller, Ranking Member Thune, and members of the Committee, thank you for scheduling today's hearing on improving cybersecurity through the NIST and private sector partnership.

My name is Mark Clancy, and I am the Corporate Information Security Officer at The Depository Trust & Clearing Corporation ("DTCC"). I also serve on the Executive Committee of the Financial Service Sector Coordinating Council and as the Vice Chairman of the Financial Services Information Sharing and Analysis Center (FS–ISAC).

DTCC is a participant-owned and governed cooperative that serves as the critical infrastructure for the U.S. capital markets as well as financial markets globally. Through its subsidiaries and affiliates, DTCC provides clearing, settlement and information services for virtually all U.S. transactions in equities, corporate and municipal bonds, U.S. government securities and mortgage-backed securities and money market instruments, mutual funds and annuities. DTCC also provides services for a significant portion of the global over-the-counter ("OTC") derivatives market. To provide insight into the criticality of DTCC's role in the safe and efficient operation of the U.S. capital markets, in 2012, DTCC's subsidiaries processed more than $1.6 quadrillion in securities transactions.

Today, I am testifying on behalf of the American Bankers Association,[1] Financial Services Roundtable,[2] and the Securities Industry and Financial Markets Association[3] who collectively represent a large segment of the financial services sector.

At the highest level, we applaud and support the goals of S. 1353, The Cybersecurity Act of 2013 introduced by the leadership of this Committee. In my testimony today I will address current cyber threats, the sector-led initiatives to defend against these threats and the ways in which the Committee bill supports those efforts. Finally, I will stress the continued importance of crafting a more robust threat information sharing environment, particularly across our critical infrastructure.

Current Cyber Threat

According to McAfee and the Center for Strategic and International Studies (CSIS), there is an estimated $100 billion annual loss to the U.S. economy and as many as 508,000 U.S. jobs lost as a result of cybercrime and cyber espionage.

For the financial services industry, cyber threats are a constant reality and a potential systemic risk to the industry. Our markets and financial networks are predicated on trust and confidence. The trusted transfers and transactions that occur hundreds of millions of times a day are a fundamental prerequisite for modern capital markets, investors, consumers, and governments to conduct business and drive economic growth.

Given the reliance on technology and the importance of for trust in the sector, individual institutions, and the industry as a whole perform risk assessments based on the types of attacks and threat actors they are subject to. The industry groups threat actors into four categories—Crime, Hacktivism, Espionage and War.

> *Crime*—The motivation of these groups is financial gain. The threat intensity of these groups varies based on two factors: the capabilities of the actors and the vulnerabilities of the targets. While organizations are continually assessing and addressing potential gaps in their systems, criminals are just as quickly acquiring new technical skills and capabilities through a sophisticated cyber black market

---

[1] The American Bankers Association (ABA) represents banks of all sizes and charters and is the voice for the Nation's $14 trillion banking industry and its two million employees.

[2] The Financial Services Roundtable (FSR) represents 100 of the largest integrated financial services companies providing banking, insurance, and investment products and services to the American consumer. Member companies participate through the Chief Executive Officer and other senior executives nominated by the CEO. Roundtable member companies provide fuel for America's economic engine, accounting directly for $98.4 trillion in managed assets, $1.1 trillion in revenue, and 2.4 million jobs.

[3] The Securities Industry and Financial Markets Association (SIFMA) brings together the shared interests of hundreds of securities firms, banks and asset managers. SIFMA's mission is to support a strong financial industry, investor opportunity, capital formation, job creation and economic growth, while building trust and confidence in the financial markets. SIFMA, with offices in New York and Washington, D.C., is the U.S. regional member of the Global Financial Markets Association (GFMA).

Hacktivism—The term hacktivism is applied to groups or individuals who use computer intrusion or "hacking" techniques to promote and publicize an often radical political or cultural point of view. The most recent example of hactivism has been the distributed denial of services (DDoS) attacks for which the Cyber Fighters of Izz ad-din Al Qassam have claimed credit. These attacks against large financial institutions began in 2012 allegedly to protest the posting of the "Innocence of Muslims" video on YouTube. This group, like virtually all hacktivists, is not motivated by financial gain—it wants to make a high-profile political statement. The capabilities of hacktivists vary greatly, although it is common to find a few highly-skilled individuals operating in loose confederation with lesser-skilled, but highly-motivated actors.

Espionage—The term cyber espionage was coined to reflect the "spy vs. spy" activity that has occurred between nations. However, cyber espionage has expanded in recent years beyond attempts to steal national secrets to now include cyber theft of proprietary information from corporations in an effort to gain an economic and competitive advantage over the commercial interests of a country.

War—This generally refers to the launch of a cyber-missile or some other cyber weapon of mass destruction to devastate the capabilities of a government or corporation by causing a physical system to fail or to gain control over that system. Today, as many as 30 countries have cyber war units to protect and defend against such an attack, according to former Secretary of Defense Leon Panetta, who also oversaw a cyber-command center comprised of Army, Navy, and Air Force personnel. In addition, some countries are developing units to promote or instigate this type of warfare.

The universe of threat actors, regardless of the category into which they fall, pose a significant and growing danger to the sector. These threats range from theft, to disruption and destruction.

Theft—Actions resulting in the theft of customer, proprietary, or confidential data or information. The loss of essential account information has the potential to put the public in harm's way for fraud and identity theft. If the crimes happen regularly, confidence in the sector could erode. The theft of a customer's access credentials when stolen via malicious software installed on the individual's computer is particularly dangerous because that customer faces the potential loss of his or her funds and assets.

Disruption—Actions intended to cause disruptions to systems and operations, denying authorized users access to the affected systems. For example, in the previously mentioned DDoS attacks against the sector, hacktivists successfully blocked or otherwise limited the availability of certain consumer-facing websites for brief periods, but did not impact any institution's internal or critical functions. In the future, more severe cyber attacks could attempt to target these internal, critical functions.

Destruction—Actions intended to compromise the integrity of or cause the destruction of data and systems.

Financial firms take extreme precautions to guard against these three main types of incidences that could impact the integrity of customer or institutional data. Not only is this an issue addressed by individual institutions' risk management functions, but also an issue that has interest by executive leadership to increase the investment in this critical space.

The Systemic Impact of Cyber Attacks on DTCC

As mentioned earlier, DTCC serves as the critical infrastructure for global financial markets. As a result, the organization brings a dual perspective to its view of the cyber risk environment and its impact on critical infrastructure. First, DTCC must examine and plan for cyber attacks that could impact its ability to perform clearance and settlement and other critical post-trade processes that underpin the global financial marketplace. Second, because of the interconnectedness of the financial system, DTCC must also take into account the broader systemic risks that could result from a cyber attack on its systems.

The global financial system is an enormous, interconnected "system of systems." In other words, while individual institutions operate different parts of the critical infrastructure, the financial system itself is a product of the interactions of all these discrete actions. Because DTCC is connected to thousands of different market participants spanning the entire financial services industry globally, the organization must look beyond how a cyber attack could harm its own operations to the systemic impact on its members and the broader financial community. For example, if DTCC is unable to complete clearance and settlement due to systems disruptions or outages, buyers and sellers of securities would not know if their trades had completed and, therefore, what securities they own or how much capital they have.

DTCC's financial risk and operational assessments must take into account these essential functions and determine how non-performance would impact the markets it serves as well as the firms that utilize its products and services, the investing public and the U.S. economy. In other words, if a cyber attack directed at DTCC, or other critical financial market infrastructure, rendered its systems non-operational, what would that do to the overall functioning of the financial system? If the financial markets could not operate, how would that affect liquidity and access to capital? This systemic view of cyber risk has driven DTCC to broaden its perspective on cybersecurity to include consideration of ways to mitigate low frequency but potentially high-impact scenarios that a monoplane risk assessment would have ignored.

DTCC maintains an elaborate and sophisticated information security program to protect against the types of cyber attacks mentioned above. This includes ongoing collaborative efforts with the private and public sectors. The financial services industry is currently engaged in a variety of public-private partnerships with the Federal government to protect against cyber threats and safeguard the Nation's critical market infrastructure.

Sector-Led Initiatves

The financial services sector recognizes the risks, views cybersecurity as a non-competitive area and works together to identify potential threats and techniques to mitigate them. A key organization to this coordination is the Financial Services Sector Coordinating Council ("Council"), whose mission is to strengthen the resiliency of the financial services sector against cyber attacks and other threats to the Nation's critical infrastructure. The organization's leadership is comprised of industry utilities and operators, as well as industry associations, such as those on whose behalf I am testifying today.

The Council is spearheading financial services participation in the discussions surrounding implementation of Presidential Executive Order 13636—Improving Critical Infrastructure Cybersecurity through the involvement of the ABA as co-chair of the FSSCC Policy Committee and SIFMA as lead on the incentives efforts.

The FSSCC Threat and Vulnerability Committee, co-chaired by the BITS[4] division of FSR, discuss the evolving threat to identify sector initiatives for mitigation. The Committee also developed a methodology for identifying core infrastructure for the sector along with the Department of Treasury.

The ABA, FSR and SIFMA are also collaborating with the U.S. Department of the Treasury, in concert with the Council, the Financial Services Information Sharing and Analysis Center and The Clearing House, in an effort to enhance the industry's cybersecurity ecosystem. The effort has led to the development of an Action Plan of both short-and long-term improvements to the sector's security posture focused on enhancing information sharing, increasing analysis, improving crisis management response and upgrades to core components of the cyber ecosystem.

On July 18, the industry participated in Quantum Dawn 2, a cybersecurity exercise organized by SIFMA. Five hundred individuals from over 50 entities throughout the sector and government participated in this opportunity to run through their crisis response procedures, practice information sharing and refine protocols relating to a systemic cyber attack. Quantum Dawn 2 was executed on a simulation platform developed as a result of cybersecurity research funding from the Department of Homeland Security's Science and Technology Directorate and was used in the exercise to simulate the U.S. equities markets. Participants are currently analyzing the findings to identify areas for improvement and best practices that will enable firms and the entire sector to better prepare for and defend against cyber threats. The exercise demonstrates the positive linkage between research and development investments, such as simulation tools, and the ability to reduce cyber related risks through preparedness that could not have been accomplished using real world infrastructures.

Lastly, some of these initiatives involve fundamental changes to the cyber ecosystem. In December 2011, the ABA and FSR formed a new entity, fTLD Registry Services, LLC (fTLD), to apply for and run industry-related top-level domains. This decision was predicated upon an announcement by the Internet Corporation for Assigned Names and Numbers (ICANN) to allow for an unlimited number of top-level

---

[4] BITS, as the technology policy division of the Financial Services Roundtable, addresses issues at the intersection of financial services, technology and public policy, where industry cooperation serves the public good, such as critical infrastructure protection, fraud prevention, and the safety of financial services.

domains (TLDs) beyond the 23 existing at the time (*e.g.*, .com, .net and .org). fTLD's goal is to represent the financial services community and to help assure that new TLDs related to the banking and insurance communities will reduce industry risk and protect customers and institutions. In addition, fTLD helps develop sound Internet practices and standards and advocates for secure Internet policies.

Legislation

We appreciate and support the goals of S. 1353, The Cybersecurity Act of 2013 sponsored by Senator Rockefeller and Senator Thune. If made into law, Title 1 of this bill would leverage the National Institute of Standards and Technology (NIST) to facilitate the necessary private and public sector collaboration to establish voluntary standards and best practices to better secure our Nation from cyber attacks.

As discussed in detail above, the sector believes strongly in the importance of private sector leadership for responding to this threat. We also recognize the need for a partnership between the private sector and the government. The government plays a unique role in the protection of private sector companies. To be successful the collaboration needs to include the leadership in the private and public sector as well as the practitioners who address cybersecurity related risks every day. The frameworks and standards that are rooted in the global, real world, and real time nature of the threat, are those that will achieve the objectives of the Nation to reduce risk from cyber threats to critical infrastructure.

The sector works closely with our government counterpart the Financial and Banking Information Infrastructure Committee (FBIIC). The FBIIC, led by Treasury and chartered under the President's Working Group on Financial Markets, is charged with improving coordination and communication among financial regulators, enhancing the resiliency of the financial sector, and promoting the public/private partnership. Essential to the sector's success is the public sector's commitment to the public/private partnership outside of the already mature regulatory regime.

The sector has participated in a number of NIST initiatives over the years and has found the organization to be ideal for the development of standards and collaboration. Most notably, the industry has been involved and continues to participate in the implementation of the National Strategy for Trusted Identities in Cyberspace (NSTIC).

Participation in the development of the Cybersecurity Framework by NIST has been a major initiative of the sector. We provided comments to NIST from the FSSCC with an emphasis on the existing national and international regulatory frameworks that the sector currently complies with. We have actively participated in the workshops and are appreciative of the specific efforts by NIST to seek the sector's input on specific topics and understand how the Cybersecurity Framework will be used by our sector.

In addition to specifying NIST as the government organization with the responsibility to develop standards, the legislation would enable critical steps for increasing research and development for the design and testing of software, educating the workforce, preparing students for future technical jobs and promoting a national cybersecurity awareness campaign. These are all critical issues to the financial services sector.

There are two points for consideration as this bill moves forward.

In the development of a research agenda, we strongly encourage you to include the evaluation of risk management throughout the supply chain. It is important for all sectors to improve their ability to detect and defend against software and hardware components that have been tampered with during production, shipment and throughout the international supply chain process. This recommendation is based on research and discussion done by the sector in the development of the Council's research and development agenda[5].

In addition, as the NIST Director establishes a cybersecurity awareness and preparedness campaign, we encourage the Director to analyze and leverage the work already underway by the National Cyber Security Alliance. This organization, supported by a number of sectors and government partners, developed the *Stop. Think. Connect.* campaign to encourage a shared responsibility across enterprises and individuals for securing the Internet.

Need for Information Sharing Legislation

We encourage the passage of the S. 1353, The Cybersecurity Act of 2013. In addition, we encourage the Senate to introduce and pass legislation that would enable

---

[5] *http://www.fsscc.org/fsscc/news/2013/FSSCC%20RD%20Agenda%20April%2024%202013.pdf*

increased cyber threat information sharing between the private sector and government, while providing the necessary privacy protections for individuals.

Our sector works collaboratively with our government partners to:

- Prepare for cyber attacks by collecting, analyzing and disseminating threat information to the extent currently feasible, assessing systemic risks, and conducting joint exercises.
- Stay ahead of adversaries and reduce the number of incidents by anticipating threats, implementing countermeasures and addressing critical vulnerabilities.
- Identify incidents as they occur by implementing key controls that would improve our ability to detect and block cyber attacks at "net speed".
- Respond to incidents in the manner that will reduce the impact and risk to the financial institution and the sector.
- Improve security posture, and minimize impact through robust forensics, investigations and learned capability.

Given the interconnected nature of cyberspace, institutions recognize that the strongest preparations and responses to cyber attacks require collaboration beyond their own companies. As a result, the sector has engaged in a number of collaborative efforts. Through the FS-ISAC, participants share threat information between financial institutions and the Federal government, law enforcement and other critical infrastructure sectors. The FS-ISAC also has a representative for the sector on the National Cybersecurity and Communications Integration Center floor to provide the Department of Homeland Security (DHS) insight into the financial sectors issues and incidents and provide an additional fan out for information from DHS to the sector.

Cyber attacks are not specific to the financial services sector, but are the concern of all targeted sectors, making it essential to be able to share threat information across sectors. Currently, we all experience attacks and work within our sectors as the law allows. Viruses, trojans and other malicious software may be written to target a specific sector, but are often developed or leveraged to attack other sectors for additional purposes. Attackers are looking for methods to increase efficiency, so their ability to reuse these tools in attacks on multiple sectors accomplishes this goal. Our attackers share information related to their attacks. American businesses defending against cyber attacks need that same capability. The ability to share information across sectors and with the government is necessary to effectively prepare, recognize and respond to attacks that hit across sectors. As our adversaries evolve, techniques become more complex, and coordinated attacks become commonplace, we need to advance our ability to respond in a collective, coordinated fashion.

The ability to share information more broadly is critical and foundational to our preparation for and response to future attacks. While we constantly review opportunities to improve the information shared within our industry, it is vital that our efforts also include sharing information across sectors and between the government and the private sector. Each company and public sector entity has a piece of the puzzle and an understanding of the threat. Our ability to share this information will greatly increase our ability to prepare and respond to threats.

Conclusion

On behalf of the DTCC and the financial services industry, I would like to thank you for holding today's hearing to continue to raise awareness on this critical issue and for inviting us to testify. I would be happy to answer any questions.

The CHAIRMAN. Thank you, sir.

Dorothy Coleman is Vice President of Tax, Technology and Domestic Economic Policy of the National Association of Manufacturers. We welcome you.

STATEMENT OF DOROTHY COLEMAN, VICE PRESIDENT, TAX, TECHNOLOGY AND DOMESTIC ECONOMIC POLICY, NATIONAL ASSOCIATION OF MANUFACTURERS

Ms. COLEMAN. Chairman Rockefeller, Ranking Member Thune, and members of the Committee, thank you for the opportunity to appear today to testify on behalf of our nation's manufacturers.

My name is Dorothy Coleman. I am the Vice President of Tax, Technology and Domestic Economic Policy at the National Association of Manufacturers, the Nation's largest industrial trade association, representing small and large manufacturers in all industry sectors and in all 50 States.

The NAM has enjoyed a close working relationship with the Committee for a number of years, and we appreciate your support and leadership on a number of issues that are important to our industry, including cybersecurity.

One of NAM's top four goals is to ensure that manufacturers in the United States are the world's leading innovators. Cybersecurity is key to achieving this goal.

We support creating a voluntary, industry-led standards development process, strengthening the cybersecurity research and development strategy inside the Federal Government, creating a highly skilled cybersecurity workforce, and raising public awareness of cyber threats. The Cybersecurity Act of 2013 represents a sensible, bipartisan, nonregulatory approach and highlights the importance of moving forward on this issue.

Manufacturers are entrusted with vast amounts of data through their relationships with customers, suppliers, and governments. They are responsible for securing the data, the networks on which the data run, and facilities and machinery they control. Manufacturers are the owners, operators, and builders of our nation's critical infrastructure, ranging from energy plants to highways. They rely on technology to design, produce, and deliver products ranging from nanoscale electronic devices to fighter jets.

The design, collaboration, and information that helped drive this innovation has moved almost exclusively online, exposing companies to cyber thieves constantly attempting to penetrate networks and steal intellectual property to replicate products and designs and disrupt business activity and critical infrastructure.

Manufacturers recognize they have to secure their networks, their controls, and their data. In a recent NAM membership survey, 96 percent of respondents said they have ongoing efforts to strengthen their information technology networks and protect their IP. More than 90 percent of the respondents have upgraded their IT assets, and more than half have hired outside cybersecurity experts.

Thus, the NAM encourages the Federal Government to advance cybersecurity preparedness through increased collaboration and coordination with the private sector. Our top priority is allowing voluntary sharing by the public and private sector of real-time threat information to allow manufacturers to better protect themselves from cyber threats.

In addition, any cybersecurity initiative should protect personally identifiable information and civil liberties and not grant the Government new authority in this realm or the ability to monitor or censor private networks.

We oppose the creation of a static, regulatory-based government regime. Potential cyber threats change rapidly and manufacturers need the flexibility to pivot quickly and defend against these threats in real time. Time spent complying with outdated and burdensome regulations will negatively impact manufacturers' ability to protect their key assets.

27

Comments by NAM members to NIST reflect their belief that any cybersecurity framework should be voluntary, risk-based, and flexible enough to keep pace with ever-changing cyber threats. Most importantly, any threat information the Government can share with the private sector will be the most effective way to combat cyber threats.

The framework also should act more as guidelines for best practices and take into account the global presence of manufacturers and related international standards in place. A major concern is that the creation of any new set of standards, even if they are voluntary, could lead to another regulatory regime and cause even more challenges to manufacturers.

We are pleased that your legislation addresses many of these challenges, and we appreciate your balanced, nonregulatory approach to reduce the risk of cyber threats based on a public/private partnership. The National Cybersecurity Research and Development Plan would further secure wireless technology, software systems, and the Internet while guaranteeing individual privacy.

We also support the creation of cybersecurity modeling and test beds to examine our capabilities and determine our needs.

We appreciate your efforts to raise the priority of cybersecurity through all agencies.

At the end of the day, however, the ability to receive real-time threat information remains manufacturers' top priority and will be the most effective way to combat cyber threats.

Manufacturers also realize that an ongoing partnership with the Federal Government is important. NAM members generally support establishing NIST as a facilitator of industry-led discussions on standards, guidelines, and best practices. Many NAM members are participating in the NIST Cybersecurity Framework discussions. Those sessions have been productive and our members want the process to continue.

At the same time, there are concerns that codifying NIST as the facilitator may somehow negatively impact the process or, even worse, give NIST the authority to recommend binding regulations. As noted before, manufacturers will not support any legislation that creates a new, overly burdensome regulatory regime.

Thus, we are pleased that creating new regulations is neither the intent or the goal of your legislation. We appreciate that your bill specifies that any recommended standards will be voluntary and will not prescribe specific technology solutions, products, or services.

In conclusion, manufacturers' ability to protect their products, processes, facilities, and customers is critical for their continued success and the broader economic security of the Nation. Your bill represents a good first step in assisting manufacturers in their ongoing efforts to reduce their cyber risk.

Thank you for the opportunity today to appear before you. The NAM looks forward to working with the Committee as the process moves forward. Thank you.

[The prepared statement of Ms. Coleman follows:]

PREPARED STATEMENT OF DOROTHY COLEMAN, VICE PRESIDENT, TAX, TECHNOLOGY AND DOMESTIC ECONOMIC POLICY, NATIONAL ASSOCIATION OF MANUFACTURERS

Chairman Rockefeller, Ranking Member Thune and members of the Committee, thank you for the opportunity to appear today to testify on behalf of our nation's manufacturers on "The Partnership Between NIST and the Private Sector: Improving Cybersecurity."

My name is Dorothy Coleman, and I am the Vice President of Tax, Technology and Domestic Economic Policy at the National Association of Manufacturers (NAM), the Nation's largest industrial trade association, representing small and large manufacturers in every industrial sector and in all 50 states. We are the voice of 12 million manufacturers in America.

The NAM has enjoyed a close working relationship with the Committee for a number of years. Mr. Chairman, we appreciate your unwavering support for the Hollings Manufacturing Extension Partnership, which has proved invaluable for small manufacturers in West Virginia and around the country working to develop the next breakthrough manufacturing technology. Thank you, too, for your leadership on spectrum issues, which are critically important to the many manufacturers that use wireless technology in their businesses.

Ranking Member Thune, the NAM and our members have worked closely with you on multiple issues. You have been a strong advocate for the close to 40,000 manufacturing employees in South Dakota on both tax and trade issues. We look forward to continuing our working relationship with you on cybersecurity and the other legislative priorities for manufacturers.

Cybersecurity has been a focus of this committee in recent years. On behalf of our nation's manufacturers and all those who want to ensure the protection of our critical assets and intellectual property (IP) and to work together with the Government to achieve this goal, I am pleased to testify on the Cybersecurity Act of 2013 and to discuss the partnership between the National Institute of Standards and Technology (NIST) and the private sector.

Overview

Manufacturing remains an important economic force in the United States, representing 12 percent of the U.S. economy. Nonetheless, despite the critical role the industry plays in the economy, taxes, legal costs, energy prices and burdensome regulations make it 20 percent more expensive to manufacture in the United States than in any other country.

The NAM's *Growth Agenda: Four Goals for a Manufacturing Resurgence in America* is a comprehensive plan to address these challenges, unleashing the economy and manufacturing's outsized multiplier effect. The *Growth Agenda* makes the case for pro-growth polices to ensure that:

- The United States will be the best place in the world to manufacture and attract foreign direct investment;
- Manufacturers in the United States will be the world's leading innovators;
- The United States will expand access to global markets to enable manufacturers to reach the 95 percent of consumers who live outside our borders; and
- Manufacturers in the United States will have access to the workforce that the 21st century economy demands.

Manufacturers recognize that we face very specific challenges in achieving these goals. In particular, in pursuing our goal to be the world's leading innovators, our industry faces constant threats from nefarious actors in cyberspace attempting to access our IP and operations unlawfully. These threats endanger our continued economic growth and safety of our citizens.

Thus, the NAM believes that we need to develop appropriate general and industry-specific best practices for improved cybersecurity. In formulating cybersecurity policy, we support a public–private partnership that draws on industry best practices.

The cybersecurity debate has moved forward significantly this year, and the business community has the leadership of you, Mr. Chairman, and Ranking Member Thune to thank for that. Your bill represents a sensible, bipartisan, non-regulatory approach to an issue of utmost importance to the manufacturing industry. Manufacturers support creating an industry-led, voluntary standards development process, strengthening the cybersecurity research and development strategy inside the Federal government, creating a high-skilled cybersecurity workforce and raising public awareness of cyber threats.

The introduction of this bill has also effectively signaled to the business community and to your Senate colleagues the importance of moving this issue forward.

There are a number of additional issues that other committees need to debate, but we are pleased with the steps you have taken.

Manufacturers and Cybersecurity

Manufacturers are entrusted with vast amounts of data through their comprehensive and connected relationships with customers, vendors, suppliers and governments. They are responsible for securing the data, the networks on which the data run and the facilities and machinery they control at the highest priority level.

In addition, manufacturers are the owners, operators and builders of our nation's critical infrastructure. They manufacture and use the temperature controls regulating the grain silos that store our nation's food supplies. They build and manage the systems operating the traffic signals that govern the rules of the road. Manufacturers make technology products ranging from nanoscale electronic devices to fighter jets. They build and run the energy plants that power our homes and businesses and the heavy machinery exploring the oil and gas fields that make America competitive.

In addition, manufacturers leverage technology to design, produce and deliver these products. Technology is also used to manage, monitor and secure key facilities and products, including trade secrets and patents.

These products, controls, systems, patents, trade secrets and all other tools that differentiate manufacturers in the United States from their competitors are the envy of the world. The movement of design, collaboration and information that helps drive this innovation almost exclusively online has created a new vulnerability: exposure to cyber thieves that are constantly attempting to penetrate networks to steal this IP. This illegal activity allows bad actors to replicate products and designs and disrupt business activity and critical infrastructure.

The stakes are high. What was once only the concern of businesses' IT departments has now become an important issue throughout manufacturing facilities, large and small. Leaders of manufacturing enterprises know they have to secure their networks, their controls and their data. In fact, in a recent NAM membership survey, 96 percent of respondents said they have ongoing efforts to strengthen their information technology networks and protect their IP to reduce their risk. More than 90 percent have upgraded their IT assets, and more than half have hired outside cybersecurity experts.

Manufacturers know the economic security of the United States is related directly to our cybersecurity. Given that our economic security is critical to our national security, manufacturers are leaders in cyber defense and are working constantly to ensure their companies, products and customers are secure.

Cybersecurity Policy

During the cybersecurity debate in recent years, the NAM has been clear on what actions we believe the government should take to address current cyber threats most effectively. We have communicated our priorities to leaders in both the House and Senate and to the White House. I am pleased to share those with you again today, and I applaud you for addressing a number of these issues over which your committee has jurisdiction.

NAM members value the strong partnership they have with the public sector and believe that partnership should extend to cybersecurity efforts. The NAM encourages the Federal government to advance cybersecurity preparedness through increased collaboration and coordination with the private sector.

In particular, manufacturers' top priority is allowing the voluntary sharing by the public and private sector of real-time threat information to allow manufacturers to better protect themselves from cyber threats. In contrast, under current law, the government is prohibited from sharing sensitive cyber threat information with the private sector. Manufacturers are hesitant to share information with the government due to liability uncertainty and exposure. Companies also are not permitted to share information freely with their peers.

The NAM supported the Cyber Intelligence Sharing and Protection Act (CISPA) of 2013 (H.R. 624), which the House passed earlier this year. This legislation, if signed into law, will allow the government to share timely and actionable threat and vulnerability information with the private sector. Mr. Chairman, as a member and former chairman of the Senate Intelligence Committee, we encourage you to work with your colleagues on that panel to address the issue of information sharing.

Manufacturers value the privacy of individuals and the need to protect personally identifiable information and civil liberties. We believe that any cybersecurity initiative the Federal government undertakes separately or in partnership with the private sector should place a premium on ensuring this information is secure. At the same time, it is important to ensure that any effort does not grant the government any new authority in this realm or give the government the ability to monitor or censor private networks.

Developing a Cybersecurity Standards Framework

The NAM believes that the public and private sector must partner closely to establish the best way to defend against ever-changing cyber threats manufacturers face. We oppose, however, the creation of a static, regulatory-based regime. This approach will not enhance cybersecurity—it will do just the opposite.

The cyber threat that now confronts all entities in both the public and private sector is commonly known as the "advanced persistent threat" or APT. Cyber hackers and thieves are changing their tactics every minute. Manufacturers need the flexibility to pivot quickly and defend against these threats in real time. Any mandatory regulations imposed on manufacturers will be obsolete the day they are published. The time spent complying and adjusting to outdated, burdensome and potentially duplicate regulations will negatively impact manufacturers' ability to protect their key assets.

Rather than develop mandatory regulations, the government should apply to the cybersecurity challenge the public–private partnership model that has been effective in other areas. While the Federal government has the resources to facilitate industry-led discussions on how best to defend against the APT, industry officials bring real-world expertise and experience unique to their segment.

In fact, NAM member companies have been on the record in their comments to NIST and in their participation in the cybersecurity framework discussions around the country that implementing any framework should be on a voluntary company-by-company basis. The framework needs to be risk-based, and it must keep pace with ever-changing cyber threats. Most importantly, any threat information the government can share with the private sector will be the most effective way to combat cyber threats.

A one-size-fits-all approach to a standards framework will not be effective. Manufacturers vary in size, come from a cross-section of diverse industry segments, have differing amounts of available resources and are exposed to external actors in different ways. These factors all will play a role in how each manufacturer implements a cybersecurity strategy. Imposing a single regulatory model would result in little or no participation in the framework. Rather, the framework should act more as a guideline and advocate for best practices. The framework must also take into account the global presence of manufacturers and all international markets in which they operate and the related international standards already in place.

The most common theme we have heard from our members is that a number of standards already exist. A major concern is that the creation of any new set of standards—even if they are voluntary—could lead to another regulatory regime and cause even more challenges for manufacturers. Any framework NIST may develop must take into account existing standards already being followed by the private sector.

Cybersecurity Act of 2013, S. 1353

The Cybersecurity Act of 2013, S. 1353, introduced yesterday addresses many of the challenges described above. Mr. Chairman and Ranking Member Thune, we appreciate your efforts to reach out to all stakeholders to create a balanced approach to reduce the risk of cyber threats to critical infrastructure based on a public–private partnership model.

The legislation would create a national cybersecurity research and development plan to further secure wireless technology, software systems and the Internet, while guaranteeing individual privacy. The legislation would also create cybersecurity modeling and test beds to examine our capabilities and determine our needs. It does all of this while ensuring coordination across the government. We appreciate your efforts to raise the priority of cybersecurity throughout all agencies.

Your bill also would place a priority on developing a high-skilled cybersecurity workforce. Through competitions, challenges and scholarships, it would create incentives to join this growing workforce at a time when our country needs it most. Most importantly, it would assess current skill sets and help determine what more is needed in curriculum and training to ensure we have the workforce we need. Manufacturers are facing a skills shortage in many disciplines, and any effort to close that gap is one we support strongly.

The national cybersecurity awareness and preparedness campaign has been well received by NAM members. Efforts to increase the cyber intelligence and cyber safety of the public and state and local governments will benefit manufacturers as they hire the workers they need and as they operate in their communities.

We have heard the most from our member companies on Title I of the bill, Public–Private Collaboration on Cybersecurity. As I stated earlier in my testimony, the ability to receive real-time threat information remains manufacturers' top priority. This will be the most effective way to combat cyber threats. Manufacturers realize that an ongoing partnership with the Federal government—in addition to information sharing—is also important.

In addition, NAM members generally support establishing NIST as a facilitator of industry-led discussions on standards, guidelines and best practices among other efforts to reduce cyber risks to critical infrastructure. Many NAM members are participating in the NIST cybersecurity framework discussions underway. Those sessions have been productive, and our members want the process to continue.

Nonetheless, they have some concerns about this approach. In particular, some companies are concerned that codifying NIST as the facilitator may somehow negatively impact the process, or even worse, give NIST the authority to recommend binding regulations.

It is our understanding that creating new regulations is neither the intent nor the goal of the legislation. We appreciate that this is referenced specifically in the bill, which requires that any recommended standards are voluntary and will not prescribe specific technology solutions, products or services. The legislation is even more specific by citing that any information shared in the standards development process shall not be used to regulate any activity of the sharing entity.

On behalf of the NAM's 12,000 members, this is a point I cannot stress strongly enough—manufacturers will not support any legislation that creates a duplicative regulatory regime that puts undue burdens on manufacturers. We are, therefore, pleased that this legislation prohibits that from happening while at the same time solidifies the public–private partnership in efforts to address an issue of critical importance to our nation.

Conclusion

In our fast-moving, hyper-competitive 21st-century economy, cybersecurity is an issue of increasing importance to the manufacturing industry. The stakes are high for manufacturers and the rest of the business community. Manufacturers' ability to protect their products, processes, facilities and customers is critical for their continued success and the broader economic security of the Nation. The legislation the Committee is examining today represents a good first step in assisting manufacturers in their ongoing efforts to reduce their cyber risk. Manufacturers must and will continue to drive the process, and a partnership with the government is a key component of the effort. The NAM supports the goals of the legislation and appreciates the Committee's efforts to address this important issue. Thank you for the opportunity today to appear before you. The NAM looks forward to working with the Committee as the process moves forward.

The CHAIRMAN. Thank you.

I should inform our colleagues that the vote starts in about 3 or 4 minutes. Senator Thune, I can stay. I will stay, or I will come back if I go vote. But if there are members, Senator Klobuchar or you, sir—if you cannot come back, then you may want to ask a question now.

Senator Klobuchar?

Senator KLOBUCHAR. I will just ask one question here at the beginning.

The CHAIRMAN. Actually, Heinrich comes before you.

Senator KLOBUCHAR. Well, there we go.

[Laughter.]

STATEMENT OF HON. MARTIN HEINRICH, U.S. SENATOR FROM NEW MEXICO

Senator HEINRICH. That rarely happens.

Dr. Gallagher, I just wanted to ask you a quick question about how—you have expounded a lot in terms of the collaboration that you have with the private sector and how critical that is. How do you also learn from the other agencies and entities that you work with within the public sector who have specific expertise in this area so that we can make sure that that then has a direct benefit on the private sector? And in particular, I know in my district you are very familiar with what Sandia does. They get about 20,000 to 30,000 attacks an hour. What is the mechanism for making sure that what we learn from some of those things makes it out into the private sector where appropriate?

Dr. GALLAGHER. So thank you. I do not know if you know—my father was a lifelong employee at Sandia National Labs and I have been out there looking at their cybersecurity work.

You are exactly right. There are two actual roles of NIST. One is the technical depth, and we have talked about that. And that is so important in terms of providing a venue to work with the private sector and be neutral.

But the other role of NIST is coordination of standards in the sense that we are sort of a corporate memory within the Federal Government about how to work with the private sector on various standard setting activities, whether it is Smart Grid in energy or whether it is cloud computing, or health care information systems.

One of the other roles we have is a very natural collaboration role with the other Federal agencies. That has been a key part of this effort as well, working with a very broad range of agencies. You can imagine, given the definition of critical infrastructure, it is basically a very large group of agencies: Energy Department, Transportation, Department of Treasury, Homeland Security, our intelligence community, and so forth. So that is a key part. This is an "all hands on deck" effort. We want to bring as many smart people as we can into the effort.

Senator HEINRICH. Thank you.

Thank you, Mr. Chairman.

The CHAIRMAN. That is it?

Senator HEINRICH. Yes.

The CHAIRMAN. Are you sure? OK.

Senator Klobuchar?

STATEMENT OF HON. AMY KLOBUCHAR, U.S. SENATOR FROM MINNESOTA

Senator KLOBUCHAR. Mr. Chairman, thank you so much for holding this hearing on this incredibly important topic.

I would like to underline the fact that cyber crime and espionage are resulting in major financial losses for American businesses. Last year, General Keith Alexander, the head of Cyber Command and the National Security Agency, said that they represent the largest transfer of wealth in human history.

Recent reports by McAfee, the Center for Strategic and International Studies estimate that the toll of cyber crime is about $100 billion per year.

Under Secretary Gallagher, what is your best dollar figure estimate of the economic toll on American business due to cyber crime and espionage?

Dr. GALLAGHER. I do not think I can improve on your estimate. So I will not hazard one.

Senator KLOBUCHAR. OK, very good.

Do you think that there are enough incentives in place for the private sector to participate in NIST's process for establishing standards? Do you think the current incentives are sufficient, or do you think more needs to be done?

Dr. GALLAGHER. So the view I have taken on the incentives question is that it is going to be easier to evaluate that when we are trying to put the framework into place. The framework is designed to be aligned with business. The goal here is to make good cybersecurity performance equivalent to good business practice. Therefore, the right way to look at the incentives question is to look at the friction as companies are trying to put this framework into place. It could be the business-to-business relationship, and we have talked about that. It could be about the risk sharing. It could be about the interaction between the private sector companies and the Government. And I think until we start getting some experience with how this framework of practices starts to go in place, it is going to be difficult to guess which of the incentive issues are going to be most important. But I think the goal is to try to make this equivalent to good business.

Senator KLOBUCHAR. Anyone want to add anything else?

Mr. COVIELLO. I would be happy to add to that.

I think there is going to be a tremendous incentive to adopt this framework. As I said in my opening remarks, as companies adopt more and more technology to improve the productivity in their business operations, they are going to expose themselves more and more to these cyber threats. So, it will be a business imperative to have the ability to defend themselves.

I think the level of not only awareness but understanding of the threat and the problem has risen dramatically in the last several years due to a number of well publicized attacks and the very figures that you quote. So I think it is going to be a matter not only of a priority for businesses but one that could even provide competitive advantage by having the best cybersecurity regime possible.

Senator KLOBUCHAR. Well, just along those lines, my last question is—I will put some more in the record. But one of the parts of this bill that I think is really important is the National Cybersecurity Awareness Campaign. Frameworks and voluntary standards are useless if our citizens do not practice cybersecurity at home, at school, at work, and I think without the public understanding and understanding the significance of the challenge, we are going to continue to be vulnerable.

Does anyone want to talk about that? Mr. Clancy?

Mr. CLANCY. I would be happy to.

So I have used a lot in my conversations metaphors because most people do not understand the technical world that I live in. The one I use in that case is around seat belts. So we have NIST that gives us a good set of specifications of what a seat belt should do, what its action should be, how you install it in the car. We also need to make sure that people are wearing them. And we are in the early days. This is cars in the 1950s where we did not have seat belts. Right? That is where we are with cybersecurity. So the combination of the good standard and the education for the public at large, as well as people who are the ones who install and fabricate seat belts—that is kind of what we need for this ecosystem that will change the physics of the problem that we suffer through today.

Senator KLOBUCHAR. Very good. And I think also I would just add that I think higher education institutions could play a role in this as well. I happen to know a few that are pretty good in my State. But I think that that would make a difference as well.

So thank you very much for your work, and I look forward to working with you, Mr. Chairman, on this bill. Thank you for your leadership.

The CHAIRMAN. Well, thank you. Do you wish to name each of those institutions?

Senator KLOBUCHAR. They know who they are.

The CHAIRMAN. You are from Minnesota. You might as well do it.

Senator KLOBUCHAR. Well, like the University of Minnesota, a small Big 10 school, or St. Cloud State.

The CHAIRMAN. OK. I have heard of it, yes.

[Laughter.]

Senator KLOBUCHAR. The Golden Gophers.

[Laughter.]

The CHAIRMAN. Mr. Gallagher, NIST and your computer security division in particular has taken on the job of establishing some very technical and complex standards over the years. I am not sure everybody on the Committee or elsewhere understands the extreme difficulty of your mission or the scientific rigor with which you approach your standards work.

Now, one of the witnesses just made a very important thing when he was talking about seat belts. He said it is one thing to develop seat belts. It is another thing to use them. And that I think trails generally along in this whole conversation.

The representative of NAM said we could not support anything where you were required to wear your seat belt, I mean, in allegory terms.

And that is troubling because all of you have been hacked into. All of us have been hacked into. I even got so desperate that I got the SEC—and now it is law—to say that every time anybody is hacked into, they have to report that to the SEC and the SEC has to put it on its Web site as a way of informing their shareholders that they better be doing something about this.

So the question of doing something about it but then actually finding out what is the best possible standard and somehow adhering to that is not inconsequential. That is not a part of what we are doing here. It is not a part of our bill. But it is something I think we have to keep in mind.

Anyway, a lot of your most complex standards are adopted worldwide, like algorithms for search engines. Could you just kind of give me a walk through, before I have to race out of here and to come back, on how do you facilitate with the private sector consensus on standards that are essential like this? How do you get it?

Dr. GALLAGHER. So the NIST role in supporting the technical side of standards setting is really derived from our measurement science roots, and they tend to have two characters to them. In some cases, a standard, a common practice, a desired practice is by its very nature very technical. It may be based in science. A good example is encryption where you need an ability to write a code using a public key infrastructure that works and has a certain resistance to attack. The answer to that is actually answered through a lot of mathematics, very complicated mathematics, to take a look and prove that performance. So this is a case where there are technically better answers and worse answers, and the job at NIST is for those scientists and mathematicians to work with the world's experts in these algorithms to look at the features of these codes and to see which ones work.

The other type of standard is actually a case where there could be several right answers, let us say, interoperability where in a certain type of transmission standard or data standard there could be one type of file format or another type of file format, and if we do not come to agreement, the systems would not be able to talk to each other and that would be a problem. In that case, it is not that the science or technology is dictating that one answer is necessarily better than the other, and it is more about getting the community of practice, the companies, together and having a discussion about which one we are going to settle on. And in some cases, what that boils down to is how will we know that we are complying with the standard, and that could be a measurement, a test. And what the NIST role will be is supporting the test that works.

So it is interesting that——

The CHAIRMAN. I am panicking a little bit here. You just used the words "settle on" and you used the word "standard." So my question is supposing everybody again being hacked into and lots of them not knowing it, doing something about it, maybe not. You get some big companies or some semi-big companies in there and you are discussing with them what could be the best approach for them. And they come very close to agreeing with each other but do not entirely agree with each other. There is a scientific sort of a miscommunication of some sort or a difference of opinion. How do you resolve that if you want to see this put in practice?

Dr. GALLAGHER. So the most straightforward way to resolve that is through a test. So I think the point that you care about in this case is the overall security performance of that system is what matters. And so what you want to do is have a testable level of performance. So in the middle of this discussion between companies, if they have different options about how to achieve that performance, the role of NIST will often be in finding out which one works better and then coming up with a test, a rigorous test that can be used to demonstrate that the standard works. And that is often what our role is in supporting that type of activity.

The CHAIRMAN. What do you do if one test works and the other company's test does not work but they both think that is what they should be doing?

Dr. GALLAGHER. It depends on the use. So if the standard is completely commercial, if this is a VHS versus BetaMax discussion and there is no public consequence, we may not do anything. Most standards in this country are in the private sector. That is what the National Technology Transfer and Advancement Act tells us to do is depend on that private sector infrastructure.

But if the performance is safety or security or something where there is a strong public sector interest, then in fact we do not have to adopt it. We do not have to use it. We do not have to recognize it. And that is one of the reasons why it is so important in these efforts, particularly in something like cybersecurity, that the public sector agencies, Federal, State, and local, are participating in this process because there is clearly a public interest here in the integrity of these systems. They would not be critical infrastructure otherwise.

The CHAIRMAN. OK.

I have got 3 minutes to go 10 minutes. So I am just going to sort of recess this for a moment, and then I will be right back. And John Thune will be right back. So we are in recess.

[Recess.]

Senator THUNE [presiding]. The hearing will reconvene.

That was a very short break. I got a feeling you guys did not get an opportunity to do much during that break. But we will try and keep it rolling so we can keep this thing on schedule and wrap up at a reasonable hour. But we do appreciate your indulgence and patience around what inevitably happens here in terms of votes.

I will direct this to you, Mr. Gallagher. I want to commend you for NIST's efforts thus far in working collaboratively with industry to address the cyber threat. We have received positive feedback from industry regarding the workshops that you have hosted and the transparency of your process.

The legislation that Chairman Rockefeller and I have introduced authorizes NIST on an ongoing basis to facilitate and support the development of an industry-led and voluntary set of standards to improve security, as we mentioned in the opening statements.

In your testimony today and previously, you have also stressed the importance of the process being industry-led. And I am wondering if perhaps you could elaborate on why an industry-led process will be successful and create, in the end, a better product.

Dr. GALLAGHER. So thank you.

I think there are three major reasons why the industry leadership is essential.

The first one Art Coviello actually touched on in his opening statement, which is the know-how and the capacity are largely in industry, and embracing that is the best way to have an agile process that in fact keeps up with this technology. It is evolving very, very quickly.

The other reason is that having an industry-led process vastly increases the chances that the answer is compatible with business. And since the goal here is to put this into use—having a standard on a shelf is not going to help anyone—then the more we can align these practices with good business practices, the types of risk management that companies do anyway, the better off this will work.

And the third reason is it can operate at the scale of markets. The Internet information technology is global, and if this is a Government-led effort, the answer we come up with is not going to be acceptable around the world probably because it was Government developed. But if industry develops it, it can be internationally used and it can harmonize efforts across markets all around the globe. And so I think from a trade and competitiveness perspective, the technologies, the solutions, the software work around the world, and that is something that would not happen unless industry led the effort.

Senator THUNE. And could you describe a little bit how you are working with industry stakeholders to ensure that the framework that you are developing with industry will be flexible, performance-based, and also cost effective?

Dr. GALLAGHER. So we are working as aggressively as we can to pull in existing practices where many of those features have been demonstrated already. And the issue of scalability—that almost forces you to have a performance-based system because the things you do in a very large, multinational corporation are going to be very different than the things you would do in a company with 5 to 10 employees. But the types of things, the performance you are trying to achieve in fact had the same goals.

And the other thing that I think is quite interesting with the evolving framework is that in addition to embracing sort of risk management—in other words, this is as much about what you do as it is about the specific technical controls or things that you do to protect systems. The other thing that is coming up is implementation levels, in other words, a maturity model, the notion that your thinking evolves. In the very beginning of the process, if you do not have a lot of experience, you may have a very rule-based or control-based scheme where these are the top things I am going to do. These are the core behaviors we are going to enforce within our company. We are going to check passwords.

But as you evolve, in fact, what happens is almost a security culture takes hold. It is about continuous improvement. It is about having the capacity to look at what is happening in your system to adjust to that, and it becomes much less about a rule following type culture and more about a continuous improvement. And that is being incorporated into this framework, which I think will really support implementation because it tells a company at the beginning of the process what they need to do and that is a different set of things than a very mature company would be looking at.

Senator THUNE. Let me just direct this question, if I can, to our industry witnesses. And I will repeat what I said. The feedback in terms of the NIST process under the EO has been generally positive. And I am curious to know what has been your involvement or your sector's involvement in the NIST process and if there is anything that you could suggest to the Committee or to NIST, for that matter, to improve that process.

Mr. COVIELLO. I would be happy to start, Senator.

First and foremost, to your point about it being industry-led, just to give you an idea of the resources that can be brought to bear, RSA hosts the largest security conference in the world. We have over 300 vendors that come to our conference every year. So you think about the scale of capability from 300 vendors that attend our conference to have an impact in terms of developing this framework with the latest and greatest, most innovative technologies.

I would also add I have never seen a period where there was more investment from venture capital and others in the space, because it is such a tough problem to solve.

So you have got that weight of knowledge. Combined with that, you have the vertical industry knowledge of their being able to evaluate the risk in their environments, how to go about implementing the right technologies in a fashion that gives you true defense and depth.

Now, on the other side of the equation, you have NIST, which has an excellent technical capability, bringing together those resources and drawing the best of it to build that framework and not doing it in a vacuum, but doing it collaboratively with both industry verticals as well as the technology companies that provide the solutions.

So this bill I think is so important because it sets the right direction to get the best results.

As to your specific question, RSA has already been working with NIST to help develop this framework. We have expertise in the areas of identity management, in big data security analytics, in encryption technology, and in building out the framework. We bring our expertise in these specific technology areas to NIST and to the body of work that is being done.

Senator THUNE. Mr. Clancy?

Mr. CLANCY. I would add to that—and I pretty much agree with all the things that Art said—that the financial sector is very invested in this process for two reasons. One, we want to make sure there is a good and productive outcome and, two, because we want to improve the capability of the other infrastructures that we depend on.

And I think the key—and I mentioned this in my testimony—is this stuff for us has to be grounded in the real world. One of the challenges with some of the standards process, not so much the way that NIST works, but other organizations is they have people who are professional developers of standards who do not live in the real world. And so from the financial sector, we had to invest our experts who know this space because we want to get productive outcomes. And NIST has been very good at taking that input from our expertise and others they have brought to bear because we want this framework to work because we want to use it to improve our cybersecurity and improve the maturity—that was another thing that was mentioned—the maturity scale of the various players in the industry. So you have large institutions operating on large scales like mine that need to be very mature. We also have a lot of small institutions who do not actually run most of their own infrastructure. We need to get the service providers that provide them the capabilities to have this level of maturity to protect the sector overall and the Nation's critical infrastructure.

The CHAIRMAN. Ms. Coleman?

Ms. COLEMAN. Senator, from the NAM point of view, this issue, cybersecurity, has become increasingly important, and it has moved up the corporate ladder, so to speak, and it is now a boardroom issue for many of our members. A lot of our members are participating in the NIST forum and find these discussions very helpful and want to see the process continue. And I think from our perspective, the fact that we are talking about industry-led, voluntary standards in a public/private partnership are really key to our support.

Senator THUNE. Thank you. I am well over my time, and I would be happy to yield to my colleague and neighbor from the State of Nebraska for any questions she might have.

STATEMENT OF HON. DEB FISCHER,
U.S. SENATOR FROM NEBRASKA

Senator FISCHER. Thank you, Senator Thune, and thank all of you for being here today. I appreciate it.

Mr. Gallagher, how will the NIST framework relate to DHS's implementation program?

Dr. GALLAGHER. Well, we hope that the implementation program that DHS adopts is all about promoting adoption of this framework. This is industry's work. We think industry will come up with something that is quite effective. And the purpose of that program should be to support those companies adopting it making it useful, whether that is through education, and the incentives and other activities in the program.

Senator FISCHER. Will NIST have any input into that process?

Dr. GALLAGHER. Yes. It has been a very collaborative activity already, both on the performance goals of the program—we have been working extremely closely with DHS. I have a weekly call with them, and at the working level, I think it is daily. That is also true on the implementation, and it is also true in the framework process because the framework process needs to be designed from the perspective of being implemented. So a lot of this discussion is already being done not just between the two agencies but in the broader effort as well.

Senator FISCHER. And I know that NIST has worked with private industry quite a bit on this. Is that correct?

Dr. GALLAGHER. That is correct.

Senator FISCHER. And do you believe there are some essential elements in there that need to be included to make this a success?

Dr. GALLAGHER. In terms of any particular area, it is actually a long list of areas that have been talked about. In fact, a big part of the framework effort is just organizing those areas into a structure and a language that everyone can collaborate under. So it talks about identification of threats. It talks about protection. It talks about response capability and recovery. And there are key activities in all of those areas. So they are all important.

I think the proof in the pudding here is when you put this all into practice, does it make a difference in the overall performance of this very complicated system that is comprised of technology people and processes.

Senator FISCHER. Do you see any specific issues that need to be prioritized within that framework? What would you suggest?

Dr. GALLAGHER. Well, we have actually turned the question around to the industry that is putting this together. So this is an industry-led effort. This is really their document. That is for us a key measure of the success.

I think that the initial framework will have sort of two characteristics. One will be a body of existing work, existing best practice that has come out of all the participating companies that become a common set of practices. The other thing that I expect to see in the framework is a set of areas that are gaps that everyone agrees needs to be addressed, but there may not be a body of existing best practices to implement.

And so the final framework will have two pieces to it: a set of best practices and I think a road map for improvement. And that is one of the reasons why the framework process cannot be a once-through. It is really important then to turn back and start working on those gap areas and use it as a road map for continuous improvement because this technology is just that dynamic.

Senator FISCHER. The framework is due in October. Is that correct?

Dr. GALLAGHER. That is correct.

Senator FISCHER. You said there will be gaps. So do you anticipate that there is going to be something written into this to acknowledge that there will be gaps and that it needs to be updated and filled in as those become more, I guess, recognized as time moves on and what is needed and working with the industry and hopefully continuing to listen to their input?

Dr. GALLAGHER. So an explicit part of the ongoing process has been identifying areas where there is broad consensus that it is a critical area but maybe that the actual technical standards that would form the basis of a response are not considered sufficiently mature. And so that is already happening. And I think the framework needs to be an honest document, and I think it needs to showcase those areas. And if it generates a prioritization—remember, you have got all of these companies working across the sectors. If they can agree that this is a priority to address, I think that is a very powerful outcome of the framework itself.

Senator FISCHER. So we all like to talk about being flexible and having flexibility no matter what the topic. In this case, then you would certainly encourage that there would be flexibility with regard to this?

Dr. GALLAGHER. I actually would go further. I would say this cannot work if there is not flexibility. The threat environment that is facing and the pace of technological change is so rapid that there has to be a dynamic environment—that is really the goal of embracing industry. It knows how to keep up with this. And that is why it is so important that they take this process and take it to scale so that it keeps up.

Senator FISCHER. Thank you very much.

Thank you, Senator.

Senator THUNE. I thank the Senator from Nebraska.

The Senator from Massachusetts, Senator Markey?

STATEMENT OF HON. EDWARD MARKEY, U.S. SENATOR FROM MASSACHUSETTS

Senator MARKEY. Thank you very much. I appreciate it.

Mr. Coviello, good to see you again. Welcome.

Mr. COVIELLO. Thank you, Senator.

Senator MARKEY. You are a preeminent leader in the cybersecurity field, and I have always appreciated your insights and we are fortunate to have you here with us today.

From Hanscom to all of the companies up in Massachusetts led by EMC, we are a leader from Massachusetts on the issue of cybersecurity, and I thank you for all the work that you have done.

When we talk about this issue, the electricity grid comes to mind. And back in 2010, I was able to author with Fred Upton a piece of legislation, informed by expert testimony from our national security experts, to put in place a set of protective policies so that our electricity grid would be difficult to attack successfully. As we all know, Thomas Alva Edison would recognize our electricity grid today. It has not been modernized the way our telecommunications system has been modernized since the 1996 Telecommunications Act. It just has not seen the kind of change.

So my question to you is since so many experts felt that the electricity grid was so vulnerable—and that can cause catastrophic damage because that affects every industry not just one—what is your feeling about that in terms of the vulnerability of the electricity system, the grid in our country today? Mr. Coviello, Mr. Gallagher, whoever?

Mr. COVIELLO. I will be happy to start, Senator. And thank you for your kind remarks.

As I think Chairman Rockefeller pointed out, there is no industry and no part of our critical infrastructure that is not in some form or fashion vulnerable to cyber attack. And why we are so positive on this legislation is the fact that it calls for industry, including the public utility industry, to bring forward their ideas on how to understand and evaluate risk and how to implement not only policies but technology to mitigate that risk. And that includes the use of technology.

What we need to do, and what should be part of this framework, is to develop a system that allows us to not just try to prevent intrusions—because they will occur, they will inevitably occur—but to be able to detect them more quickly and respond quickly enough to mitigate any potential harm.

Senator MARKEY. Can I just ask you a question?

Mr. COVIELLO. Sure.

Senator MARKEY. Because my time is going to run out here.

I released a report about 2 months ago on the electric grid's vulnerability to a cyber attack, and about 100 utilities responded to Mr. Waxman and myself. What their responses revealed was that there is ongoing attempts to go after our electricity grid. But the responses revealed something else which is that the utilities were almost all fully compliant with the mandatory standards that the industry develops and the Federal Energy Regulatory Commission enforces but none of them reported compliance with the voluntary recommendations made by the North American Electricity Reliability Corporation, an industry group that develops these measures.

So I know that the utility sector is not the same as the industrial sectors that we are talking about today, but the utilities are already subject to mandatory reliability standards, and keeping the lights on in the face of a cyber attack is fundamental reliability.

So I would be interested in your views on this tension between carrots and sticks because it is pretty clear that in the utility sector, they do not respond to voluntary, only to mandatory. Could you give me your insight in terms of what you think we have to put on the books to get that kind of a response?

Mr. COVIELLO. Well, again, I think the bill that is before this committee—I do think is the right approach. I think you would have to speak directly to them about their ability to volunteer.

But I think, again, what we are trying to accomplish here is to give them the means and the capability in the form of this framework to be able to defend themselves. And I cannot emphasize enough the fact that the technology is moving so quickly that having a framework that is flexible and adaptable that keeps pace with not only the threat, but the expansion of the attack surfaces is going to be critically important.

I will also state that the problem is likely to get worse before it gets better. As we create what we call the "Internet of things"—in other words connecting more and more physical devices to the Internet—then the attack surface is going to expand even more dramatically. And we have to have capability to address that.

So my role here today is to comment on this legislation and how effective I think it would be in giving the private sector the means to protect the critical infrastructure. And I think it is the right path.

Senator MARKEY. Do you see any additional incentives that we could include to encourage adoption of voluntary standards?

Mr. COVIELLO. I think that there could be other considerations. I cannot, off the top of my head, give you examples today, but it would be something that you could consider.

Senator MARKEY. So in other words, a backup capacity. So we have learned that the electric utility industry does not, in fact, implement voluntary standards, only the mandatory. So would you support some backup standard that if there was no compliance and it has been identified as a critical area that needs protection, that there has to then be some mechanism to ensure that there is an adoption?

Mr. COVIELLO. Well, again, I do not speak specifically for the industry, but I think if they were given the right framework—and that is what we are attempting to do with the executive order and with this bill—I think it will go a long way to having them see the light to adopt this framework.

Senator MARKEY. But if there is no adoption, in other words, should there be—because of the critical nature of this threat to our country, should there be a mechanism to ensure that there is compliance because we are only passing this because we have identified a threat?

Mr. COVIELLO. Well, it is always in the purview of Government to do what is right in the public interest. So under that scenario, I would not rule anything out.

Senator MARKEY. OK.

Mr. Chairman, thank you. I appreciate it.

The CHAIRMAN [presiding]. Thank you, Senator Markey. I understand exactly what your thrust is there. I have to say as chairman, I share some of that, but that is not actually within our jurisdiction and we have to sort of live with that. I mean, this is the voluntary, working with industry. The questions you asked are completely understandable and I think in the long run necessary, but that is what Homeland Security does.

Senator MARKEY. I see.

The CHAIRMAN. You see?

Senator MARKEY. I was operating under the misimpression that you were chairman over everything that comes under the purview of private commerce in the United States.

[Laughter.]

Senator THUNE. I would say to the Senator from Massachusetts the Chairman likes people to think that.

[Laughter.]

Senator MARKEY. Thank you, Mr. Chairman.

The CHAIRMAN. Oh my God.

[Laughter.]

The CHAIRMAN. Dr. Gallagher, you negotiate with world groups on standards. So now, we have been talking here about—let us say we have got standards on American cybersecurity and what do we do about all of that. You negotiate with world organizations, and you do it over the same kind of thing. What do you do when you arrive at differences, substantial differences? If you do not understand my question——

Dr. GALLAGHER. I think so.

The CHAIRMAN.—please say so and I will try again.

Dr. GALLAGHER. So the international standards process is actually one where NIST does not represent the United States. Again, since we have an industry-based standard setting process in this country, our presence in international standard setting is set by those private sector standards organizations. What we try to do is facilitate that process. And a lot of that has to do with making sure that the best technical answer is supported. You know, we would prefer effective standards over ineffective standards.

But I have to say the most effective role in international standard setting is the role of companies, particularly international companies, because they have a stake already in these multiple areas. And in fact, it is that desire to have as common a market as possible that is a big influence in those areas. So the key to international standard setting—it is always a complex issue—is participation, and it is one of the reasons why I think this framework process is so important. By coming together and developing a common set of practices, we will shape what international standards look like. That tyranny of the first draft and shaping what this looks like really matter. And I think we already see signs of other countries, other areas. Whether they are going to be voluntary or whether those countries decide to go into a regulatory approach, they are already interested in basing whatever they do on what is already happening here in this framework process. And I think that is a good thing because the more we get common behavior and common practices, the more compatible this enterprise is with the way business works.

The CHAIRMAN. In a sense what we are doing is we are asking you to develop standards that are effective standards that will really improve our country's cybersecurity in a voluntary fashion. We are not asking you for window dressing or for a proposal to make every single stakeholder happy. That was sort of a dumb last sentence. But it is a very big responsibility because you want to be effective. You do not want to be sort of a United Nations between competing ideas and people come to this point and then they stop, so they cannot close, so they do not do.

Are you and the rest of the NIST staff committed to the goal of developing effective standards, and how would you answer that differently than I asked you a previous question? How do you come to agreement? The word "effective," as Senator Markey indicates, is important.

Dr. GALLAGHER. I think it is absolutely critical.

The way I think about this question is we are talking about a set of activities owned and operated by the private sector that if they were to fail through a cyber attack would have catastrophic impact to the country. That is the definition of critical infrastructure that is in the Executive Order. So there is clearly a national interest in that not happening. And so effectiveness is actually the starting point. This has got to work.

I think the position we take is that if we can make this work, working through industry in a market-centric way, in a way that adapts all of the capacity they have, all of the adaptability they have and aligns with business practice—and that is an "if." If that works, that is the best answer because it can scale internationally. It can keep up with the technology, and there is this little sort of counter-market things that we have to do. If it does not work, I think the question before Congress will be what do we do about that because you still have a national impact.

So the position of NIST has been this has got to be effective. It has got to address lowering the overall risk of these types of failures. And it has to be measured by being put into practice and it has to continually get better because both the threats are going up and the technology is changing, and the nature of the vulnerabilities are shifting. So it has to be continuous.

The CHAIRMAN. Yes.

Senator Thune, can I ask one more question?

Senator THUNE. Yes, sir.

The CHAIRMAN. OK, because I am over my time limit.

I mentioned before that because you could not get anything done in legislation—we were not getting anything done in legislation and that this in fact—even national security—I mean, so much braid and stars you cannot even believe it. Masses of it, acres of it begging us to pass legislation that will make cybersecurity attacks much more hard or that we can stop them. Now, you suggested one way, but you did not suggest it in the way I am going to say it. But if you have a catastrophic attack, it is sort of like a 9/11 effect. People perk up and say, oh, gee, we should have prevented that. And then we pass, to the everlasting shame of the U.S. Congress, a bill.

The first thing we did after 9/11 was pass a bill which allowed the FBI and the CIA to talk to each other. I voted for the bill and then I went and blushed. I mean, it was so embarrassing we would have to do that. But that is the way it is. People do not talk to each other. They do not talk. There are stovepipes in Government, stovepipes in industry, people not wanting to get an advantage taken of them.

So I came up with this idea—Mary Schapiro was in charge at the time at the SEC—in two areas. In the matter of hacking, that the companies by definition are probably not going to say, hey, guess what, we were hacked and then send that announcement out to all their shareholders. But in an era of transparency and for the betterment of that company, their shareholders have a right, I would think, to know that their company had been hacked into. I wrote to Mary Schapiro and asked her to work on this. And it works. Now people are startomg tp report. Shareholders are seeing.

I did the same thing with coal mines. You cannot get coal mine safety legislation through this Congress with a red State. It just will not happen. Extremely frustrating. And then you live in a coal State and you see people getting killed. And, you know, coal companies like others are sort of distant and hidden and they have their own world, their own ways. And so I got her to do the same thing. If you had a coal mine accident, you were required to report that on the SEC website. And I am not saying it had a startling effect, but it had a good effect because people, in a sense, in a raw way that did not require law, were informing their shareholders that safety problems were extant and no more than that. No more authority to do anything than that, just transparency, which I think we generally are trying to believe in.

Now, I do not know how to make a question out of what I just told you. But I think you understand what I am saying. I am implying that companies sometimes have to be caused to do what they would really want to do. But I do not want the people of West Virginia to know bad things about me, which of course do not exist.

[Laughter.]

The CHAIRMAN. But should they, I do not want them to know about it. Right? Senator Thune is the same way. Well, he is more perfect.

[Laughter.]

The CHAIRMAN. But you understand what I am saying. I mean, this is a serious problem that we are getting at, and we have unclear jurisdiction over it, just like I told the Senator. But my mind just forces me to put that question to you.

Dr. GALLAGHER. So I certainly appreciate the important role that disclosure has in this environment, but since I am not an expert on those types of incentives, let me answer the question a little bit more generally.

You are exactly right that this will not do any good if it is not put into practice. And so the crux of the issue—and I think this will be—and the administration believes this is going to be the essence of the discussion we want to have with Congress as this unfolds. As the framework is put into practice, what are the reasons why it does not go into practice? Is it the motivation of the boards? Is it business-to-business transactions, where there are barriers to information in transactions? There are dependencies between companies as well. There are dependencies between the private and public sector. I believe that there is a lot of self-interest to doing this well. I think that these technology systems actually cut right to the heart of the competitiveness and viability of the companies themselves. So I think a lot of self-interest is already there.

But the extent to which we identify friction, that really should be what informs all of the subsequent discussion about incentives. And our view is that this will become very natural as we start to implement the framework, and it really becomes about an implementation question.

The CHAIRMAN. Peer pressure evolves in various ways. Is that what you are saying?

Dr. GALLAGHER. Yes.

The CHAIRMAN. OK.

Senator THUNE. Mr. Chairman, I just appreciate very much the testimony of these folks today, and I think that it helps inform our process going forward. And I guess if there is a takeaway for me—and perhaps if you all want to, just in the form of a closing comment—is that the only way that this works is if the framework really is good business and makes sense. So that is kind of what I have derived from what I have heard you say today.

I think that our bill is headed in the right direction based on what I have heard you say today. And there are other committees, as the Chairman said, that have other jurisdictions who will have to be heard from on this. And we hope that the work that they do can complement what we have done here.

But we appreciate very much your being here, and if anybody has anything they would like to close with—it is just down to us. But thank you so much for your time and for your expertise.

The CHAIRMAN. Any closing thoughts?

Mr. CLANCY. So, again, I would like to thank you for having this hearing. I look at this as an important first step. There are more steps to follow. And I think, Chairman Rockefeller, what you were getting at in terms of disclosure is a way to inform the debate about the risks that we face. The other side of that equation, as I mentioned earlier in my testimony, is around information sharing. And I think there is work for other committees in the Senate to push that forward. And the two together will be stronger than either one of those things on their own.

And I thank you again for the opportunity to speak on behalf of the American Bankers Association, the Financial Services Roundtable, and the Securities Industry and Financial Markets Association. Thank you.

The CHAIRMAN. Thank you.

Ma'am, do you have anything?

Ms. COLEMAN. Yes. Just in conclusion, I just want to reiterate that the NAM supports your legislation as introduced. We certainly very much appreciate the industry-led, voluntary standards non-regulatory approach and the public partnership that is incorporated into the legislation. And we look forward to working with you to advance this legislation. And thank you for the opportunity to testify today.

The CHAIRMAN. Thank you.

Now, I want to point out that Senator Thune, who is a smooth operator, just almost took the legs out from under me there in sort of bringing this to a close because Senator Richard Blumenthal aggressively approached me on the Senate floor on an absolutely ridiculous vote—absolutely ridiculous vote, but it was very close so it was not ridiculous—and said that he was going to be here in 2 or 3 minutes and I am so informed. So it is a question of your tolerance of the whole concept of the legislative branch of Government, if you can stand it for 2 more minutes. He is very, very smart. He was Attorney General of Connecticut for 29 years. And he wants to be here. And so if you are willing to stay, he would be very happy and I would be very happy. I mean, 2 minutes. I mean, you can handle that. You are all young.

Mr. COVIELLO. Mr. Chairman, I did not get an opportunity to make a closing comment. So maybe I can bridge the gap a little bit here while we are waiting.

The CHAIRMAN. OK.

Mr. COVIELLO. So, first of all, RSA was attacked in 2011 by two separate advanced persistent threat groups that we believe to have come from a nation state. Without the requirement of SEC disclosure, because it had not been put through as yet, our parent company, EMC, once we realized we had a loss, which was within hours of the actual exfiltration of information, we filed an 8-K report to the SEC. I also wrote an open letter to all of our customers informing them, as we had a moral obligation. So we take no credit for doing the right, moral thing to inform our customers that because of our breach, that they might have been in danger. As a result not only of our internal capability to see the attack and being a whisker from stopping it altogether, we were able to give remedial advice to our customers. And as a result, no customer suffered a loss as a result of our breach.

The point I guess I would like to make is that, first and foremost, focusing on outcomes should be an important element of our cybersecurity strategy. I think Senate bill 1386 in California about notification of breaches of personally identifiable information has caused a significant shift in how the retail industry approaches cyber. But it is not about regulating specific action about how industries go about protecting themselves. If you focused on an outcome, very often you will get industry to do the right thing.

I think your legislation is very important because it gives industry the tool to do that right thing. And I think this is a tremendous start. And, again, I want to thank you and Ranking Member Thune for your leadership because this is I think a tremendous start and an important element of protecting our critical infrastructure.

The CHAIRMAN. Good. And I agree with you incidentally.

Please, Senator Blumenthal, get here.

I agree with you because it starts with the proper framework. This is not regulatory. NIST is not regulatory. NIST brings people together, public and private. It has been brilliantly successful at that. One of the most agencies in all of the Federal Government. So it puts that forward as the ideal. In that we are going to, hopefully, get our bill passed, it will allow that to proceed.

But you are probably already proceeding on that. Are you not?

Dr. GALLAGHER. Yes. We are proceeding under the framework.

But from our perspective, we also appreciate this bill because it clarifies what are existing, but very broad authorities to do this. And in particular in light of the fact that we believe this effort needs to be ongoing and continuous, that clarification support I think is very helpful in helping to ensure that this evolves toward an industry-led program that has these features we have talked about of being agile and keeping up.

The CHAIRMAN. Our prayers have been answered and the good Senator from Connecticut has arrived.

48

STATEMENT OF HON. RICHARD BLUMENTHAL, U.S. SENATOR FROM CONNECTICUT

Senator BLUMENTHAL. Thank you, Mr. Chairman. I am going to tell my wife that she can say that when I come home tonight whether she thinks it or not.

[Laughter.]

Senator BLUMENTHAL. But thank you very much for giving me this opportunity—I really appreciate it—on a topic that is supremely important. I just came from the floor and I apologize for anyone who has been delayed.

First of all, my thanks to the chairman and the ranking member for remaining committed to finding solutions to this very real and urgent threat. Often when the legislative process fails to function properly or breaks down, people walk away and ignore the problems that still need solving, and that has not happened here fortunately. So I am heartened that the leadership of this committee has found a way to work together, and I want to pledge that I will continue to stay engaged and involved and help in whatever way I can.

I continue to be concerned with ensuring that civil liberties and personal privacy are protected and safeguarded throughout this process. My colleague, Senator Markey, has been very much focused on this issue, and I want to thank him for his work on it before he came here.

And I am also focused on making sure that we have the right incentives, the proper incentives to ensure that companies are complying with the standards.

I have a question that has perplexed me as a representative of a State which has some of the greatest companies in the world. Under Secretary Gallagher, why has the market not better dealt with the cybersecurity threat? During the financial crash, we learned about systematic risk and banks that believe they were too big to fail, to use a somewhat hackneyed, overused term. Do you think the infrastructure companies believe that the Federal Government will bail them out in the event of a catastrophe? Is that why they are not taking steps on their own?

Dr. GALLAGHER. So I would actually start by challenging the premise a little bit. I think the evidence that I have observed with companies from the various sectors coming into the process is that in fact there is a lot of actually quite outstanding activity going on. The financial services sector is a good example of one which has been under extreme duress with extremely high levels of targeted attacks to that sector and yet has really been quite good at working across company lines, sharing technical information, working with Internet service providers, working with the public sector in crafting and adapting to that pretty dynamic response.

Senator BLUMENTHAL. And I apologize, first, for interrupting you, second, because my question was unclear. I was really talking about insurance. I come from a State that has been engaged in trying to combat the cyber threat. I have talked to a number of the CEO's and lower ranking executives about their concern. But insurance does not seem to be a commonly used option. And in the normal situation in the marketplace, insurance would be a measure of how grave the threat is, everything from hurricanes and flooding to theft to—well, I do not need to tell you. Why not in this area?

Dr. GALLAGHER. So I apologize for——

Senator BLUMENTHAL. No. It was my——

Dr. GALLAGHER. So I think you are right. Certainly one of the incentive discussions is around insurance and why that market—what could be done to develop that. One of the possible reasons has to do with the fact that you need to monetize the risk. And so this comes down to measuring and understanding and sort of developing an actuarial basis where this risk can be sort of embedded in the market. This discussion has come up actually quite frequently in the framework process, and I think as part of the metrics discussion, this is something that is being looked at as something that would be quite helpful.

Senator BLUMENTHAL. And why has it not happened? The threat has been here. And I invite any of the other panelists to weigh in. But the threat has been here for well long enough to monetize and do the actuarial accounting. And in fact, in other areas I am familiar with some of the work done on climate disruption and the threat of hurricanes. Actually the insurance companies are very mindful about potential threats of hurricanes in the Northeast which are about as difficult to monetize as I would guess cyber threats are, in fact, more so because we know the cyber threat is there. We know some of the damage that can be caused. So maybe others can enlighten us.

Mr. COVIELLO. Actually, Senator, I would disagree. I actually think the cyber threat is harder to create an actuarial table or an algorithm around. And the problem is twofold. It is not just the threat environment which continues to escalate every single day in terms of capabilities of the attacker, it is the attack surface. I get asked all the time why can you guys not do a better job. Well, we could do a better job if IT infrastructures were static. They are not.

Just think about the following facts. The iPhone did not even exist until 2007. Six years later, we now have full mobile ubiquity. We use very few Web applications to run our businesses as recently as 2005 to 2007. Now a common refrain is "there is an app for that." In another 6 or 7 years, we will be using big data applications to monitor everything about us and the world around us, hopefully for productive reasons.

The amount of digital content being created every year is absolutely astounding. There was a quarter of a zettabyte—and I will explain what a zettabyte is in a moment—of digital content being created in 2007. This year there will be two zettabytes. By 2020, there will be 40 to 60. One zettabyte is the equivalent of 4.9 quadrillion books. That is the amount of content that needs to be sorted through to figure out what exactly needs to be protected, as opposed to what is a picture of your family dog.

So the complexity of protecting this fast changing IT environment is overwhelming. That is why this framework is so important. We need a security model that has legs. We need a security model that is future-proof. That model consists of starting with a thorough understanding of risk that is an ongoing process. It includes technologies that can react to facts and circumstances that are not static. It includes a management system that uses capabilities that are only just coming to market now that can spot the faint signal of an attacker. The one thing we have going for us in defending against cyber attacks is, ultimately, the attacker will have to do something anomalous. We are developing the capabilities to be able to spot that in progress. So, again, Senator, as you suggest, it is not a question of whether or if we will be breached. It is our ability to respond and detect the attacks and respond timely enough to quarantine the element of our infrastructure that has been attacked or to prevent the movement of critical information or a transaction.

Mr. CLANCY. And if I could add to that. As you know, insurance at its core is about risk transfer. So I transfer the risk that I have to somebody else who can absorb the risk. And in order to do that, you have to have two things. You have to have an understanding of the risk and the purchaser of the policy and the issuer of the policy both have to be able to value it. And I would argue that one of the challenges you have particularly in cybersecurity is that many of the people who face the risk do not have a good estimation of what it really means to them and what the consequences could be and the likelihood or frequency of those events occurring. And that is one of the reasons why I believe the information sharing component, which is not addressed in this bill, is another tool in the toolbox to help us understand that risk better.

We use cyber risk insurance, but we use that cyber risk insurance at DTCC for the risks that are smaller. The catastrophic risks that we could face if these issues escalate to a point where they become manifest are really beyond the ability of the insurance industry to absorb right now. And so we have to look at making sure that those things do not occur.

Senator BLUMENTHAL. You know, I understand what you have said, and I do not disagree with it, that it is a moving target, so to speak, that it is not a static threat with sort of inert, chess-like moves that are fully visible and are played according to the same rules all the time forever. But that is the nature of insurance to try to look forward and put numbers on risks that may vary and may change over time.

So I am still perplexed. I do understand what you are saying, and I wonder, if I can ask a question, whether it is the fact that the insurance would be too costly because of the factors that you mentioned or because the insurers simply do not want to be in that market. They just do not want to even engaged or be involved in offering that product.

Mr. COVIELLO. Again, Chairman Rockefeller said it at the outset, that almost every agency of the Federal Government says how strategically important the nature of this threat is to the U.S. economy and our defense.

So I would say that over time, if we are as effective as I think we will be, I think we can get to a point where we can reach an equilibrium, where we are not playing the attackers are one up against us and we are trying to catch up and react to the threat, that we are able to develop a system that is resilient enough to not necessarily stop any loss, but to respond quickly enough. And at that point, I think the cost curve will come down sufficiently that you will be able to insure against this problem.

Senator BLUMENTHAL. I think your points are very well made. And in my view, they are great evidence for the need for this legislation.

Mr. COVIELLO. No question.

Senator BLUMENTHAL. Because here is an area where normally the private sector would say we will take care of it. We know you are the Federal Government and you are here to help, but we can do it on our own. Here the markets, or the insurance market at least, cannot really satisfactorily address the incalculable threats, the magnitude of the harm, and other factors that you have put so well.

Mr. COVIELLO. Thank you.

Senator BLUMENTHAL. My time has expired, but I want to just say on the issue of privacy and civil liberties that I think that the draft legislation from Senator Rockefeller and Senator Thune includes language that instructs the director of NIST to—and I am quoting—include methodologies to protect individual privacy and civil liberties. I hope if I can direct questions in writing to you on this area, we can get some responses from you.

Again, my thanks for being here today.

Thank you, Mr. Chairman.

The CHAIRMAN. Thank you, Senator Blumenthal.

And now I have really got to say a heartfelt thank you for your patience. I mean, we had this incredible sort of Broadway-like performance—an art form of waiting for Senator Blumenthal.

[Laughter.]

The CHAIRMAN. And Jay Rockefeller tried to ask an intelligent question and then keeping my ear open to was that door opening or not and you were coming through to save us all. And you did, indeed. But most importantly, I think some of the best testimony came within the last 10 minutes.

Senator BLUMENTHAL. Well, thank you, Mr. Chairman. and thank you for making your rebuke so soft.

[Laughter.]

The CHAIRMAN. No, no.

All right. With all certainty, this hearing is adjourned.

[Whereupon, at 4:29 p.m., the hearing was adjourned.]

APPENDIX

PREPARED STATEMENT OF HON. DAN COATS, U.S. SENATOR FROM INDIANA

Thank you, Mr. Chairman, and let me start by commending you and Senator Thune for your bipartisan leadership on the cybersecurity issue, and by congratulating you on the introduction of S. 1353, the Cybersecurity Act of 2013.

In a post-September 11 world, Americans have learned to be more vigilant. We've learned that in a second—the act of one terrorist—or a group of terrorists—can wipe away life as we once knew it and change our world forever. And so since that fateful day in September almost 12 years ago, our Nation has made great strides to be ever more vigilant and more prepared to prevent or respond to another terrorist attack.

Local law enforcement, TSA, FBI, Homeland Security and the intelligence community, among many others, must work every second of the day to anticipate, prevent and disrupt potential plots by terrorists. But these threats are changing form. It is not only a potential hijacked plane or a bomb plot that threatens our country; we now face another type of warfare that could have a deep and widespread impact on Americans—a cyber attack.

As a member of the Senate Intelligence Committee, Senate Commerce Committee and Ranking Member of the Senate Appropriations Subcommittee on Homeland Security, I know that the threat of a cyber attack is real and far-reaching. A major attack on our cyber systems could shut down the critical infrastructure that allows us to run our economy and protect the safety of Americans—transportation and financial systems, communications systems, electric grids, power plants, water treatment centers and refineries.

The threat of a cyber attack is growing, but neither industry nor government alone can broadly improve our nation's cybersecurity. This potentially devastating vulnerability requires all stakeholders to work together to develop an enduring legislative solution. Protecting Americans from cyber attacks should not be a partisan issue.

That is why I believe it is imperative that Congress pass cybersecurity legislation this year given the grave threat of these attacks against our government and key sectors of our economy. An Executive Order from the White House simply cannot provide the statutory authorities and protections needed to address the serious danger posed by cyber attacks.

The Commerce Committee will have the opportunity soon to set the tone for the cybersecurity debate by moving the ball forward in a business friendly, bipartisan way by passing the Cybersecurity Act of 2013.

Although only a narrow approach, this legislation is a good step in the right direction. It strikes the appropriate balance and preserves the private sector's leadership in the development of innovative technologies to respond to cybersecurity threats.

Bipartisan support for this legislation provides a path forward and sets an example for the other relevant committees. I am confident, for instance, that the Chair and Vice Chair of the Intelligence Committee will soon finish work on legislation to break down legal barriers and incentivize information sharing, an essential component of improved cybersecurity. There is broad, bipartisan consensus on the Committee to do just that, and I trust the leadership and flexibility demonstrated by Senator Rockefeller will be repeated by Senator Feinstein.

This legislation also provides the Senate Majority Leader guidance on how NOT to repeat the mistakes of last Congress. We really hit a low point last summer when the Senate Majority Leader rushed a cybersecurity bill to the floor under strained circumstances.

One-fifth of the U.S. Senate—both Republicans and Democrats—met every day for nearly two weeks to iron out our differences on cybersecurity legislation. And with the active participation of 20 Senators representing both parties and key committees of jurisdiction, we came close.

Several Republican and Democratic Senators had an understanding on how to best move forward on cybersecurity, and a shared commitment to work through last August toward a compromise legislation that could pass the support of both parties.

(53)

This agreement was important because throughout the consideration of this bill, the Majority Leader circumvented the legislative process and refused to allow any amendments.

Unfortunately, rather than allowing the process to advance and amendments to be considered, the Majority Leader and the White House shut down debate, forced a vote they knew they would lose and blamed Republicans for the failure. This was completely disingenuous and poisoned the well last year for progress on this critical national security issue.

The Senate should address cybersecurity this year, but not in the "take it or leave it" manner the Majority Leader has pursued in the past.

Instead, it should be done in a manner that ensures our security, encourages the voluntary participation of the most innovative aspects of the private sector and the government, and does not harm our economy.

This legislation starts us down that path. As a member of the Senate Commerce Committee and the Senate Intelligence Committee, I remain committed to working on legislation that strikes the right balance between strengthening security and respecting the privacy rights of Americans.

The responsibility falls on all of us. We know this threat is ongoing and real. We know we need to act. We must cast aside partisanship and put the security of our country above political expediency.

RESPONSE TO WRITTEN QUESTIONS SUBMITTED BY HON. MARK WARNER TO DR. PATRICK D. GALLAGHER

Question 1. On February 13, 2013, President Obama signed Executive Order 13636, "Improving Critical Infrastructure Cybersecurity," and the and the White House released a related Presidential Policy Directive (PPD–21), both of which work to strengthen the cybersecurity of critical infrastructure in the U.S.

The Executive Order directed NIST to work with industry and develop the Cybersecurity Framework, and the Department of Homeland Security (DHS) to establish performance goals. DHS, in collaboration with sector-specific agencies, is charged with supporting the adoption of the Cybersecurity Framework by owners and operators of critical infrastructure and other interested entities through a voluntary program.

Legislation recently introduced by Senators Rockefeller and Thune reinforce these executive directions, tasking the National Institute of Standards and Technology (NIST), in coordination with the industry, with developing a set of standards and best practices to reduce cyber risks to critical infrastructure.

What does NIST see as the biggest challenge in developing standards for sectors in cybersecurity. Is each sector progressing to meet the targets outlined in the President's timeline, and if not which sectors are most at risk?

Answer. NIST did not develop standards as part of its work under Executive Order 13636. Rather, NIST was directed in the Executive Order to work collaboratively with stakeholders to develop a voluntary framework—based on existing standards, guidelines, and practices—for reducing cybersecurity risks to critical infrastructure. As part of the framework development process, NIST sought public input to develop a compendium of existing sector-independent and sector-specific standards, guidelines, practices, and other informative references to assist with cybersecurity implementations.

The Executive Order specified that adoption of the Cybersecurity Framework is voluntary. As such, NIST is not working to assess sector progress. However, NIST is working collaboratively with the Department of Homeland Security to promote wide adoption.

Section 9 of the Executive Order directed the Department of Homeland Security (DHS), in consultation with sector-specific agencies, to identify critical infrastructure at greatest risk. DHS would be pleased to provide a briefing on the entities identified through implementation of Executive Order 13636.

Question 2. The standards and best practices developed through this process, as outlined by the Executive Branch and Senators Rockefeller and Thune, must be voluntary. Do you agree that the standards set by NIST should be voluntary? If not, please explain why.

Answer. NIST agrees that use of the Cybersecurity Framework and any associated Standards should be voluntary.

Question 3. How will these voluntary standards be implemented? For covered industries that already have a regulator, how does NIST assess the progress of their efforts to create standards for those sectors?

Answer. The Cybersecurity Framework will identify areas for improvement that should be addressed through future collaboration with particular sectors and standards developing organizations. As part of this process, NIST will continue to work with industries and sectors in existing standards developing organizations to address any identified needed areas.

Because implementation of the Framework is voluntary, the process by which standards may be adopted by participants will vary. The Framework is intended to be a resource, not a regulation. Sector-Specific Agencies coordinate with the Sector Coordinating Councils to review the Cybersecurity Framework and, if appropriate, develop implementation guidance or supplemental materials to address sector-specific risks and operating environments.

Question 4. How has NIST increased staffing and experience to be able to handle a large and complex project? Have government furloughs due to sequester delayed the timeline or made it more difficult to achieve the intended result?

Answer. NIST has achieved the objectives and goals assigned in the Executive Order. NIST is continuing to work with the private sector to evolve future framework versions and ways to identify and address key areas for cybersecurity development, alignment and collaboration.

Question 5. While the actions of the Executive Branch are a step in the right direction, there are still regulatory gaps that leave our Nation vulnerable to cyberattacks. Do you believe that the Cybersecurity Act of 2013 (S. 1353), recently introduced by Senators Rockefeller and Thune is effective in filling these gaps? If not, what are your recommendations for legislative action that should be taken to strengthen America's cybersecurity?

Answer. NIST is encouraged by the attention, interest, and concern within both the executive and legislative branches of government to address pressing cybersecurity challenges.

Question 6. NIST's initial steps towards implementing the Executive Order included issuing a Request for Information (RFI) this past February to gather relevant input from industry and other stakeholders, and asking stakeholders to participate in the Cybersecurity Framework process. Given the diversity of sectors in critical infrastructure, the initial efforts are designed to help identify existing cross-sector security standards and guidelines that are applicable to critical infrastructure.

How will NIST ensure that we are working across sectors to promote information sharing? I know that you held a workshop, but will there be some type of clearinghouse where information sharing can take place across sectors?

Answer. NIST works with Federal agencies and private sector companies to develop underlying standards and best practices that are used to support a wide array of information sharing activities. These standards and best practices are a fundamental component of providing interoperability between organizations, allowing for rapid and accurate sharing of information between government and industry, and industry to industry. The collaborative development approach ensures that the needs of all sectors are adequately addressed, leading to an information sharing ecosystem that benefits all organizations.

Question 7. The Department of Defense (DoD) has led a successful voluntary information sharing program that allows participating entities to gain access to cybersecurity solutions. Has NIST engaged DoD and other agencies in the National Security space to gain lessons learned to implement during their establishment of voluntary standards?

Answer. NIST works with the Department of Defense and other Federal agencies to share information, experiences, and lessons learned relating to the development of and use of voluntary standards.

Question 8. As NIST is contemplating a new cybersecurity framework for all critical infrastructure industries, the energy sector has significant questions about how this will be implemented. Cybersecurity in the power sector has been regulated by the North American Electric Reliability Corporation (NERC) for a long time. NERC administers Critical Infrastructure Protection (CIP) Reliability Standards. CIP requires implementation of specific cybersecurity protections, and subjects industry to penalties for noncompliance. Regulators are also trying out new ways of preserving cybersecurity. NERC and FERC—the Federal Energy Regulatory Commission—are supplementing their role as enforcement agencies and taking on more voluntary outreach activities, including the sharing of cyber threat information.

The Executive Order requires NIST to develop a "cybersecurity framework" for all critical infrastructure industries, but it seems unclear as to how NIST will interact with the NERC's existing standards. How will you ensure that the new standards complement existing cyber protections for the electricity sector and do not add new regulations or rules that would contravene existing programs?

Answer. The Executive Order directed the National Institute of Standards and Technology (NIST), a non-regulatory agency, to lead the development of a framework to reduce cyber risks to critical infrastructure. NIST worked closely with stakeholders from all critical infrastructure sectors including the Energy Sector, NERC, the Federal Energy Regulatory Commission (FERC) and the Department of Energy (DoE). Regulatory agencies will use the Cybersecurity Framework to assess whether existing requirements are sufficient to protect against cyber attack. If existing regulations are insufficient or ineffective, then agencies must propose new, cost-effective actions based upon the Cybersecurity Framework. Regulatory agencies will use their existing process to consult with their regulated companies to develop and propose any new regulations, allowing for a collaborative process.

RESPONSE TO WRITTEN QUESTION SUBMITTED BY HON. MARK WARNER TO ARTHUR W. COVIELLO, JR.

Question. On February 13, 2013, President Obama signed Executive Order 13636, "Improving Critical Infrastructure Cybersecurity," and the and the White House released a related Presidential Policy Directive (PPD–21), both of which work to strengthen the cybersecurity of critical infrastructure in the U.S.

The Executive Order directed NIST to work with industry and develop the Cybersecurity Framework, and the Department of Homeland Security (DHS) to establish performance goals. DHS, in collaboration with sector-specific agencies, is charged with supporting the adoption of the Cybersecurity Framework by owners and operators of critical infrastructure and other interested entities through a voluntary program.

Legislation recently introduced by Senators Rockefeller and Thune reinforce these executive directions, tasking the National Institute of Standards and Technology (NIST), in coordination with the industry, with developing a set of standards and best practices to reduce cyber risks to critical infrastructure.

While the actions of the Executive Branch are a step in the right direction, there are still regulatory gaps that leave our Nation vulnerable to cyber attacks. Do you believe that the Cybersecurity Act of 2013 (S. 1353), recently introduced by Senators Rockefeller and Thune is effective in filling these gaps? If not, what are your recommendations for legislative action that should be taken to strengthen America's cybersecurity?

Answer. This legislation complements the President's Executive Order by codifying the important steps the Administration has already taken to protect critical infrastructure and gives government and industry additional tools to bolster our cyber defenses. We are pleased to see that S. 1353 requires a voluntary, non-regulatory process, enabling further collaboration between the public and private sectors to leverage non-prescriptive and technology-neutral, global cybersecurity standards for critical infrastructure. We also commend the Committee for including crucial provisions to support cyber research and development; increase awareness of cyber risks; and improve cybersecurity education and workforce training.

It is imperative that Congress addresses other key cybersecurity issues not under this Committee's jurisdiction. These include advancing the sharing of cyber threat intelligence between government and industry; establishing liability protections for entities that share threat information; and streamlining acquisition of technology. We urge the Congress to examine ways to break down barriers to information sharing and create incentives for the public and private sectors to work together to safely and securely share real-time, actionable information about cyber threats. Linking the adoption of cybersecurity standards to incentives such as liability protection and streamlined acquisition of technology will create a positive business climate while improving our Nation's cybersecurity posture. We also support additional legislative initiatives to update criminal laws and penalties; enact Federal data breach law; modernize Federal Network Security continuous monitoring efforts; and develop reasonable and effective policy approaches to supply chain protection that will not stifle innovation and competition.

RESPONSE TO WRITTEN QUESTION SUBMITTED BY HON. MARK WARNER TO MARK G. CLANCY

Question. On February 13, 2013, President Obama signed Executive Order 13636, "Improving Critical Infrastructure Cybersecurity," and the and the White House released a related Presidential Policy Directive (PPD–21), both of which work to strengthen the cybersecurity of critical infrastructure in the U.S.

The Executive Order directed NIST to work with industry and develop the Cybersecurity Framework, and the Department of Homeland Security (DHS) to establish performance goals. DHS, in collaboration with sector-specific agencies, is charged with supporting the adoption of the Cybersecurity Framework by owners and operators of critical infrastructure and other interested entities through a voluntary program.

Legislation recently introduced by Senators Rockefeller and Thune reinforce these executive directions, tasking the National Institute of Standards and Technology (NIST), in coordination with the industry, with developing a set of standards and best practices to reduce cyber risks to critical infrastructure.

While the actions of the Executive Branch are a step in the right direction, there are still regulatory gaps that leave our Nation vulnerable to cyber attacks. Do you believe that the Cybersecurity Act of 2013 (S. 1353), recently introduced by Senators Rockefeller and Thune is effective in filling these gaps? If not, what are your recommendations for legislative action that should be taken to strengthen America's cybersecurity?

Answer. S. 1353, the Cybersecurity Act of 2013 provides some of the needed legislation for protecting our Nation's critical infrastructure and complements the February 2013 executive pronouncements.

To continue to protect our nation's infrastructure, we must pass cyber threat information sharing legislation. This legislation must provide liability protection for the sharing of threat information, allow for sharing among the private sector and from the government to the private sector, build upon existing relationships and protect personal privacy. While the financial sector has been engaged in information sharing for a long time there are still many institutions in our sector and other critical infrastructure sectors who are constrained in their ability to share due to liability concerns.

Given the interconnected nature of cyberspace, institutions recognize that the strongest preparations and responses to cyber attacks require collaboration beyond their own companies. As a result, the sector has engaged in a number of collaborative efforts, which would be enhanced with the passage of information sharing legislation.

Through the Financial Services Information Sharing and Analysis Center (FS–ISAC), participants share threat information between financial institutions and the Federal government, law enforcement and other critical infrastructure sectors. The FS–ISAC also has a representative for the sector on the National Cybersecurity and Communications Integration Center floor to provide the Department of Homeland Security (DHS) insight into the financial sectors issues and incidents and provide an additional fan out for information from DHS to the sector.

The ability to share information more broadly is critical and foundational to our preparation for and response to future attacks. While we constantly review opportunities to improve the information shared within our industry, it is vital that our efforts also include sharing information across sectors and between the government and the private sector. Each company and public sector entity has a piece of the puzzle and an understanding of the threat. Our ability to share this information will greatly increase our ability to prepare and respond to threats.

———

RESPONSE TO WRITTEN QUESTION SUBMITTED BY HON. MARK WARNER TO DOROTHY COLEMAN

Question. On February 13, 2013, President Obama signed Executive Order 13636, "Improving Critical Infrastructure Cybersecurity," and the and the White House released a related Presidential Policy Directive (PPD–21), both of which work to strengthen the cybersecurity of critical infrastructure in the U.S.

The Executive Order directed NIST to work with industry and develop the Cybersecurity Framework, and the Department of Homeland Security (DHS) to establish performance goals. DHS, in collaboration with sector-specific agencies, is charged with supporting the adoption of the Cybersecurity Framework by owners and operators of critical infrastructure and other interested entities through a voluntary program.

Legislation recently introduced by Senators Rockefeller and Thune reinforce these executive directions, tasking the National Institute of Standards and Technology (NIST), in coordination with the industry, with developing a set of standards and best practices to reduce cyber risks to critical infrastructure.

While the actions of the Executive Branch are a step in the right direction, there are still regulatory gaps that leave our Nation vulnerable to cyber attacks. Do you believe that the Cybersecurity Act of 2013 (S. 1353), recently introduced by Senators

58

Rockefeller and Thune is effective in filling these gaps? If not, what are your recommendations for legislative action that should be taken to strengthen America's cybersecurity?

Answer. The Cybersecurity Act of 2013 (S. 1353) represents a sensible, bipartisan, non-regulatory approach to an issue of utmost importance to the manufacturing industry. Manufacturers support creating an industry-led, voluntary standards development process, strengthening the cybersecurity research and development strategy inside the Federal government, creating a high-skilled cybersecurity workforce and raising public awareness of cyber threats.

The NAM is pleased that this legislation prohibits the creation of a duplicative regulatory regime that would put undue burdens on manufacturers while at the same time solidifies the public–private partnership to address an issue of critical importance to our nation.

The top priority of manufacturers is allowing the voluntary sharing by the public and private sector of real-time threat information to allow manufacturers to better protect themselves from cyber threats. In contrast, under current law, the government is prohibited from sharing sensitive cyber-threat information with the private sector. Companies also are not permitted to share information freely with their peers.

The NAM encourages the Senate to consider legislation similar to the Cyber Intelligence Sharing and Protection Act (CISPA) of 2013 (H.R. 624), which the House passed earlier this year and was supported by the NAM. This legislation, if signed into law, will allow the government to share timely and actionable threat and vulnerability information with the private sector.

○

www.ingramcontent.com/pod-product-compliance
Lightning Source LLC
Chambersburg PA
CBHW082113070326
40689CB00052B/4622